Historical Celebrations

HISTORICAL CELEBRATIONS

A Handbook for Organizers
of Diamond Jubilees, Centennials,
and Other Community Anniversaries

Keith Petersen

Foreword by J. Sanford Rikoon

Idaho State Historical Society
Boise, 1986

791.624
P484

This handbook was supported in part by a grant from the Association for the Humanities in Idaho, a state-based program of the National Endowment for the Humanities. The conclusions and opinions expressed in this handbook are the author's and do not necessarily represent the views of the Association for the Humanities in Idaho or the National Endowment for the Humanities.

Library of Congress Cataloging-in-Publication Data

Petersen, Keith.
  Historical Celebrations.

  Bibliography: p.
  1. Anniversaries — Handbooks, manuals, etc.
  2. United States — History, Local — Anniversaries, etc. —
  Handbooks, manuals, etc. I. Title.
  AS7.P46 1986   791'.624   86-7244
  ISBN 0-931406-13-7

Book design by Fred Fritchman

Second printing, 1996,
by the University of Idaho Press, Moscow, Idaho 83844-1107

ISBN: 0-931406-13-7

Printed in the United States of America

Contents

Foreword

C elebrations of shared personal, religious, occupational, and historic events are worldwide and ancient phenomena. In the United States most people participate, as either major or minor actors or members of the audience, in private events marking the human cycle and life experiences, from birth and birthdays to weddings and anniversaries to death and memorial services. We are also increasingly involved in larger group activities that commemorate such aspects of our lives as ethnic allegiances, religious memberships, occupational associations, and community, state, and national anniversaries. Truly, the diversity of the American people and their special interests is reflected in the variety of celebrations and festivals occurring throughout the country.

One common element unites all of these celebratory activities: the focus on shared group attitudes, beliefs, experiences, and events. Because group activities typically include a number of participants and public events, they generally serve wider social and cultural functions, linking members of a group to each other and to a broader segment of the public. Historic anniversary celebrations, which include events as different as the American Bicentennial and a small town's diamond jubilee, fall into the category of group events in that they are public activities inspired by a desire to honor shared perceptions of a historical past.

In this handbook, Keith Petersen provides a variety of practical details, suggestions, and models for organizing historical celebrations. His words and ideas derive both from his own widespread experiences working with community groups throughout Idaho and eastern Washington and from other organizers of past events in the same region. A careful consideration of his instruction and examples will lead any motivated community to a successful celebration, whether a plan calls for a single introspective event or weeks or months of diverse scheduling activities.

Chapter 1 focuses on organizational considerations, including the choice of a celebration date and theme, formation of necessary steering and subcommittees, planning of time schedules and activities, and the establishment of goals. These are pre-event chores that to a great extent are responsible for the celebration's content. They also determine whether or not the event will run smoothly and utilize effectively the range of resources available in any community.

Fundraising, that often mysterious task so essential if the designed program is to fulfill all expectations, is the topic of Chapter 2. Well-designed historical celebrations are events that many segments of a local community will support, each in its own most appropriate manner. There are also a host of regional, state, and national organizations that might be approached. To ensure adequate fiscal and material support, Petersen emphasizes the crucial necessity to approach individuals and organizations with a carefully considered plan that combines the needs of the event with the means and expectations of possible contributors. He also calls for a variety of fundraising activities before and during the commemorative celebration.

Chapter 3 approaches the heart of the celebration through presentation of short-term and long-term activities that are potential components of commemorative events. The menu is lengthy, the choices are difficult. Yet this breadth indicates the ability of celebrations to include virtually every form of cultural expression and presentation, from the arts to videotape shows. The uniqueness of each event arises from the nearly infinite possibilities of combining these activities. Every community also has the opportunity to flesh out each component with a form and content appropriate to local resources, skills, and traditions.

Chapter 4 is devoted to publicity, that aspect of a public event which, along with fundraising, presents the most perplexing problems to organizers. While community celebrations are special occasions of only infrequent occurrence, audiences do not automatically show up without a healthy push from effective media presentations. Petersen discusses the use of various media, ever mindful that the content of the publicity must be considered in tandem with appropriate timing, frequency, and contexts of presentation. Effective publicity requires the participation and support of those professionals in radio, newspapers, advertising, television, and the like who know the proper procedures and forms.

If organizers plan and publicize well-conceived activities, and collect adequate funds to support their programs, their celebrations should be successful. The title of Chapter 5, "Documenting the Celebration, Concluding the Celebration, and Building on What You Have Begun," denotes the fact that while historic celebrations often emphasize the past, the event's setting is the present and its consequences are felt in the future. In other words, although an event's immediate impact is a measure of momentary success, the potential of the celebration to influence future generations and events determines its lasting impact. As Petersen notes, documentation ensures that the lessons of the celebration do not die with the temporal close of the event. A careful record serves as a precedent for organizing future events, in itself becomes part of the community's historical record, and is an educational tool to extend the celebration into the future.

Instructions on planning celebratory activities can be regarded as simple hype if it lacks evidence of the value of its lessons and procedures. In Chapter 6

sketches are provided of past community events in the Idaho towns of Rexburg, Wallace, and Jerome. These capsule descriptions are important as more
than success stories. In the variety of activities, community size, organization,
and research, one notes the unique nature that each celebration assumes because
of differences in local history, participants, and resources. No other community event will be exactly the same as any of these three examples, yet any organizer
should be able to make useful comparisons, and even steal an idea or two, from
the experiences of others.

Before proceeding into sections on the "how" of historic anniversary celebrations, however, it is useful to consider some of the rationales for embarking
on ventures that will surely tax the energies and resources (and perhaps the
patience) of the active organizers. The remainder of this foreword briefly probes
the "why" of historic celebration; touches on some of the components that
link historic anniversary events in general; and suggests some functions that
community celebrations can perform, in the hope that organizers will have a
more complete idea of the significance of these special occasions. Above all,
they should remember that the impact of such celebrations is on three levels:
individual participants, the host community, and spectators from outside the
immediate group.

An event can, of course, be justified simply because "Clearville is 75 years
old" or "Idaho is approaching its 100th birthday." Anniversaries themselves,
however, are only initial motivations; it is the consideration of how and why
we celebrate that influences the particular nature of each group's activities.
No two events are exactly alike: each is shaped by a group's concept of celebration, the intended social, cultural, and economic impacts; and the differing
nature of each community's perceptions of its past. For the sake of consisten-
cy, our focus is on the type and scope of activities known popularly as "town
celebrations." Although each family or community group can arrange its own
event (and by 1990 Idahoans will witness large regional and statewide efforts),
individual communities, towns, and cities are likely to carry on the bulk of
historic anniversary celebrations.

There is no doubt that the number of community celebrations has increased
significantly over the past twenty years. This trend is as evident in Idaho as
in New Jersey, as common among ethnic groups as among religious congregations. Two major factors account for this development: the accelerating pace
of social and cultural change during this century, and the recent movement
towards local history and local action.

A familiar bumper sticker in Idaho proclaims a belief professed throughout
the state: "Idaho Is What America Was."[1] This sentiment is not exactly based
in any identifiable reality in Idaho or the Northwest. Rather, the region's population has participated in the communication, transportation, and technological
revolutions affecting the entire nation over the last hundred years. Some

developments, such as railroad building, became widespread in the Northwest years after similar evolutions in the East and Midwest. This temporal gap has not prevented the reception of these advances, nor has the "time lag" persisted. Today, advances and new trends started anywhere in the country or world are immediately recognized, and have immediate consequences, throughout the region. Moreover, no area or state has escaped significant changes, evident not only in overt examples on the cultural landscape but also in shifts in attitudes, values, and beliefs. The pace of change appears to quicken in geometric progression, leaving even individuals of the "baby boom" generation following World War II with the feeling that today's society is very unlike that in which they faced the conflict over the Viet Nam War or the introduction of the computer.

The sense that continuity cannot be taken for granted, and the knowledge that the experiences of previous generations are not at all inherently familiar or comprehensible in the context of contemporary life, supply special purpose to opportunities for historic celebration. How, in the face of what appears to be a movement towards standardized and homogenized culture, can a community define, express, and retain its own identity? An obvious answer is history, and especially local history. Here, each community can point (usually with pride) to a unique combination of personalities, events, and impact on the immediate environment. Just as some educators promote oral history interviewing as a means for individuals of different generations to learn from one another, so also can historic anniversary celebrations point to techniques for forging a special chain linking the historical periods of a community's development.

The desire and need to discover (or rediscover) and maintain community identity is related to, and likely an underlying motivation for, the recent emphasis on local studies. This development has affected scholars in academic settings,[2] but it is even more evident in the remarkable proliferation of local historians, historical societies and museums, and efforts at community historic preservation and interpretation. If communities have become more aware that much of their present-day identity can be found in their historical past, they are also becoming increasingly confident of their ability to document, preserve, and present their own heritage. Workshops, conferences, and other public events sponsored by the Working Together Project and the Idaho State Historical Society, for example, have attracted increasingly larger numbers of participants. More important, perhaps, local projects themselves are becoming broader in their range and scope, with the commemoration of historic events only one of many kinds of activities throughout the state.[3]

A comparison of the national anniversaries of 1876 and 1976 vividly depicts a broadly based changing concept of the way Americans choose to identify their own place within the national fabric. National activities in 1876 centered almost exclusively in Philadelphia. The centennial exhibitions there covered 236 acres and included five major halls — the largest named, appropriately enough, the Main Building. Possibly the largest structure in the world at that time, the Main Building was 1,880 feet long and 464 feet high and enclosed 936,000 square feet of exhibit space. The other buildings were only slightly less imposing. To this grand spectacle, touted as the biggest, fanciest, most awe-inspiring show on earth, the nations of the world and the states in the Union sent their exhibits. A gala event it was, but hardly a celebration accessible to, or reflective of, the experiences of the diverse peoples living in the United States. The Oregon State Legislature, for example, earmarked $4,000 to be utilized for an exhibit in Philadelphia. The Oregon contribution included sixty-three varieties of preserved Oregon birds, thirteen types of grass seeds, and thirty-three examples of wood specimens. But it is doubtful that many Oregonians saw their state exhibit. "It was hard work to make the people feel it was to be their exhibition," the Oregon Centennial Commissioner noted.[4] Small wonder, since the display was installed 3,000 miles from their homes and included little about the human side of Oregon history.

By 1976 celebratory ideas had changed, even in Philadelphia. The commission appointed to outline the city's plans for the Bicentennial affirmed: "Ways must be found for all sections of the country to directly participate in the celebration and not just watch events occurring elsewhere."[5] The American Revolution Bicentennial Commission echoed this thought: "Each community has its own part of the story to rediscover, to put on display and to share with neighbors and visitors alike."[6] Communities across the country did find their own appropriate settings and events, from the tall ships in New York to a Nordic Festival in Seattle and in countless parades, exhibits, and celebratory activities in towns everywhere in between. Truly, the Bicentennial was a more pluralistic celebration than the 1876 event—and one more accurately representative of American society.

While the Bicentennial provided a motivation for national celebration, local attention often settled on events and activities with few emotional associations to contemporary Americans, particularly those residing in areas such as Idaho that were little more than blank spaces on colonial maps. I do not imply that we overestimate the importance of the Lexington battle in American history, or the Declaration of Independence to the democratic process; but the Bicentennial was typically more a promotion of national than of regional or local identity.

Conversely, community historic anniversary celebrations may be categorized as public attempts to define a *community's* identity through the selection, representation, and interpretation of past historical episodes pertinent to that area, and activities designed to promote cohesiveness among immediate participants as well as to present a "historical message" to outsiders. This concept includes the two major aspects of commemorative events suggested in the phrase "historic celebration": "historic" implies the focus of the event and the content of the activities, while "celebration" connotes the actual activities. When the anniversary is the nation's birthday, the content naturally leans toward national experience and character; in 1989 and 1990, when six Northwest states are celebrating centennial anniversaries, the focus will likely be on state and regional developments. As each town passes through silver anniversaries, diamond jubilees, and the like, the nature of the activities becomes primarily local in scope. This pattern does not demand blind adherence. Indeed, in 1989 and 1990 it is hoped that each community celebrating the Montana, North Dakota, South Dakota, Washington, Wyoming, and Idaho centennials will focus only a minor part of its energy on statewide issues. The centennial occasion can be used as motivation for understanding the impact of state developments on local life and experience. Community cycles sometimes reflect larger state cycles but often they progress at different rates or even reverse the broader patterns.

"Celebration" suggests active preparation and public events. In this sense, the events are manifestations of activity and design, of purpose and goals. Among the tasks of preparation and organization, the central focus of this handbook, two aspects deserve special attention: the inclusion of all important community constituencies and the wider use of local traditions. The best community events entail the cooperative participation of all those social and cultural groups whose historical experience has played an important role in local development. In many cases these groups may not be considered part of the recognized institutional structure and may not have recognized spokespeople within the organizations normally charged with planning historical celebrations. Yet if the diversity of a community, including ethnic settlement and cultural differences, is in part responsible for the individuality of that community, then it follows that a successful expression of local history requires the involvement of all constituencies. How effective would a Pocatello celebration be without the participation of Native Americans, Mormons, and other important cultural groups in Bannock County? Can Mountain Home's celebrations be truly comprehensive without the involvement of both the civilian and the military community?

Although not often considered a motivation for celebratory events, an important dimension of historical commemorations is their impact on the organizers themselves. Few community-wide events would be possible without active participation and sharing among organizers, designers, scholars, media professionals, and many others. At least three positive results can come from bringing together people of different cultural backgrounds to work on a single project. First, the event serves as a way to break down stereotypes of each group's history through the need to accurately represent past experiences. Second, the level of intergroup rapport generally rises through both the process of shared historical research and the requirement to cooperate on the practical aspects of organization and planning. While community historic celebrations are not a social cure-all, a more complete comprehension of another group's history often leads to an increased respect for that group. Third, the sequences of planning and preparation can serve as a training ground for those less experienced in historical research, interpretation, and display. Commemorative celebrations may thus be used as a context within which knowledgeable community residents transmit their skills and ideas. Individuals gaining new ideas, insights, and abilities may then join established organizations as active participants or lead their own groups in historical projects.

The celebration of local traditions in historical anniversary events adds to both the quality and the impact of activities. For example, anyone who has witnessed a number of celebrations and festivals knows that one component of a successful event is the totality of the experience. In these situations we are afforded not only the visual delights of a parade or pageant but the smell and taste of foods, and the sounds and performances of musicians. The bombardment of our senses, in contrast to piecemeal presentations, can provide a total — albeit brief — immersion in local culture, an experience from which we derive a more complete feeling for the lives of the participating groups. Every region has the opportunity to design such a multifaceted event. If activities reflect local traditions and involve area presenters, cooks, musicians, and the like, the event will better involve a cross-section of residents in accurate portrayals of their own cultures.

As public displays, celebrations are also an interpretive tool. Every community must give careful thought to how and why certain elements of its collective past have been selected for presentation while other aspects are overlooked or consciously ignored. As anthropologist Frank Manning notes: "Celebration is a distinctive part of the cultural repertory through which a people gain perspective on their situation."[7] While the content of anniversary activities can represent a single dominating individual's perceptions of the past, events more often reflect the awareness of a group or community about itself. The activities occurring throughout the celebration period, from photo displays to parades to softball tournaments, are "messages" from and about the community. The event as a whole includes shared statements about perceptions of the past; it also acts as a message concerning future aspirations and expectations. One need only spend a short time at Orofino's Lumberjack Days, or witness Outpost Days in Murphy, to understand that public celebrations such as these are important as occasions for expressing an identity and sense of purpose.

The historical commemoration extends the basic notion of town celebration because it provides central emphases that serve to focus attention on some basic questions of identity. These questions may include why we live in a particular community and in certain kinds of houses, engage in certain occupations, have specific religious and political beliefs, and perpetuate local customs and traditions. The comment of anthropologist George Metraux, although focused more on national than on local celebrations, applies: "Traditional feasts and festivals constitute, symbolically, a way of recalling origins — whether mystical or historical — of a community of men. They are occasions when cultural and national identity can be reasserted and feelings of self-awareness and participation in common experiences reaffirmed."[8]

There is a saying among one Amish group in central Missouri that "In every blessing there is a curse, and in every curse a blessing." One blessing of historical anniversary celebrations seems to me to be the opportunity to interpret the past for public consumption. This same point, however, may be a curse in that the public nature of celebrations immediately suggests that whatever is witnessed will also be judged — very possibly by outsiders who may misunderstand or misinterpret. Thus these events can be risk-taking experiments, for the selection of a "historic face" to present to the community at large and to outsiders reveals not only perceptions about the the past but also present-day expectations and, more subtly, plans for the future.

The fact that historical celebrations are public events has ramifications often overlooked by their organizers. Having observed a number of both small and large historical anniversary celebrations over the past decade, I have noticed a relationship between the nature of these events and the composition of the audience. While to some degree the size and make-up of the audience cannot be known until activities take place, the kinds of events planned, their organization, and publicity about them shape audiences. For example, well-publicized events such as parades, pageants, and crafts exhibitions held on summer weekends are likely to attract greater numbers of outsiders. On the other hand, talks and discussions, or small-scale events held on weekday evenings, will probably have a largely local attendance.

Petersen discusses audiences and publicity pragmatically in this handbook. There are some additional links, however, between the type of targeted audience and the sense of a community about its celebration that should be kept in mind. Events directed toward larger audiences not necessarily of local origin tend to raise a sense of "otherness" and self-awareness on the part of the major participants. The presence of a majority of outsiders brings to a community an audience largely unfamiliar with local custom and attitudes. Naturally, in this case insiders react by being more deliberate in their public displays and tend to produce activities with a generalized content appropriate to the mixed audience. Smaller locally attended affairs are generally more relaxed and informal, because of the closer relationships between participants and audience and the lessened need to present an expected "face" to outsiders. In Missouri this contrast is particularly evident in the Ozark regions, where the "hillbilly" expectations of tourists are met in leisure/recreation centers. Life in Ozark towns more isolated from tourists reflects the cultural and social diversity that exists beneath this "tourist face." Organizers of wholly local events can afford not to worry about an audience's evaluations or the impact of public displays; however, there is an overall correspondence between a rise in "outsiders" and an increase in formality, self-awareness, and popularized behavior, as opposed to the likelihood of a more informal and inner-directed content at purely local affairs. Most events, of course, fall somewhere between these poles.

As a rule, there is an understandable tendency for groups to celebrate those personages, events, developments, and experiences that connote positive attitudes and beliefs about their community. Few of us are willing to honor the more controversial aspects of our existence. But our interpretations of historic components as negative or positive change over time. Fifty, or even twenty, years ago, portrayals of the ouster of Native American populations might have emphasized the speed and effectiveness of removal. Today there is a sense of collective Anglo-American embarrassment over the treatment of Idaho's original inhabitants. I would suppose that no northwestern community can comfortably find contemporary cause to include reference to physical or spiritual hostilities toward Native Americans, or Hispanic Americans, or other ethnic groups. How does one justify mentioning embarrassing events or wrongdoings? These items are often enough overlooked in printed histories, and to perpetuate their memory in public contexts appears to many to be ill-founded.

These sentiments are logical, and I do not wish to suggest that any community focus a celebration on the "darker side" of its history. Yet it is important to consistently remind ourselves that one educational function of public display is the use of the past to better prepare for the future. All celebrations have this component, whether they include active school participation or more passive instruction through the presentation of pageants, parades, or public re-enactments. While there is no way to change history, it is possible to understand its implications. If we can fully understand why particular events occurred, including the factors leading up to them and their consequences, we might be better able to prevent such experiences from happening again. We might also allow ourselves to undergo a kind of community catharsis in which we relive certain experiences not to enjoy or take pleasure from them, but rather to expunge our curiosity and gain a clearer perspective on the future.

Now that I have considered some of the sobering aspects of historic anniversary celebrations, let me note one final function of celebration: to have fun. Sadly, it too often happens that organizers and participants (and audiences) forget this important feature of communal gatherings. Indeed, my favorite definition of celebration is straight from Webster: "celebrate: to demonstrate grateful and happy satisfaction in (as an anniversary or event) by engaging in festivities, indulgence, merrymaking, or other similar deviation from accustomed routine."

While this handbook will likely not satisfy one's need of recipes for indulgence, Petersen does emphasize that dull celebrations are a chore for everyone involved. As chroniclers of celebrations around the globe have noted, the time of celebration is a time when participants are given "licence" to break their everyday routines.[9] When else can one impersonate a long-deceased ancestor or local figure, dress up like a member of a different group, or make fun of living community personages?

Historic commemorations need not deny opportunities for spontaneity, creativity, and even a little fantasy. To some degree we can borrow from the contemporary popular trends of role-playing games common among many children between ten and fifteen years of age. In games like Dungeons and Dragons and Wizardry, participants construct a play world of characters, events, and experiences according to well-defined rules. I think that kids (and some adults) have found here an appropriate blend of truth and fantasy, of play and ritual. They have a sense of authenticity, of role, and of proper behaviors. Yet at the same time the knowledge of role-playing, a component often included in historical celebrations, allows the opportunity for individual variation and expression.

Acting, role-playing, and impersonations are important activitities that serve important functions, available during community celebrations. They enable participants to "feel" history, to step inside past lives and events beyond the intellectual portholes afforded by printed documentation. Pageants, plays, historical reenactments, and other similar activities are not real time machines, of course, but they are useful attempts to experience the past with the heart and body. One cannot remove the artifacts and attitudes of the present to fully recreate the past, but perhaps they can be suspended for a short time. In this vein we have much to learn from the "living history" movement, the groups of blackpowder enthusiasts, and the twentieth-century mountain-man groups.[10] An afternoon spent shocking grain by hand as part of a display of historic agricultural techniques, or an evening with the electricity turned off as an aspect of a school project, provides brief moments of more total immersion into the past.

Historical anniversary celebrations have at least four important characteristics. First, they are shared performances and presentations of culturally meaningful events and symbols. They are not reflective of the total history of a community but reveal perceptions of the past deemed significant by the participants. Second, historical celebrations are public events, and as such are open to the evaluation and education of both the community at large and outsiders. Third, they typically involve a number of active participants from the community. This interaction not only promotes relationships within the local area but also ensures that the resultant activities will reflect a greater cross-section of the community. Fourth, celebrations must be both entertaining for the participants and entertainment for the audience. Providing stimulation for fun — even if it involves the temporary suspension of normal rules — attracts attention and participation, while at the same time it allows for the expression of attitudes and behaviors significant to each community.

J. Sanford Rikoon
Columbia, Missouri
March, 1985

NOTES

[1]That outsiders and the popular media also support this idea is most recently indicated in an article by Gregory Jaynes, "In Idaho: Living Outside of Time," *Time* (January 14, 1985), 125:8, 10.

[2]A succinct summary of the local history movement within the academic context is provided in Lawrence DeGraaf's introduction to *Interpreting Local Culture and History*, edited by J. Sanford Rikoon and Judith Austin (Boise: Idaho State Historical Society [in press]).

[3]Perhaps the best overviews of these activities are contained in the accumulated issues of the *Idaho Oral History Center Newsletter*.

[4]See *Report of the Centennial Commissioner, A J. Dufur, to the Legislative Assembly* (Salem, Oregon: State Printer, 1878).

[5]*The Philadelphia Plan and Report of the Officers: A Proposal for the Bicentennial Celebration of the United States and an International Exposition in Philadelphia in 1976* (Philadelphia: The Philadelphia 1976 Bicentennial Corporation, 1968), p. 30.

[6]*Community Rediscovery '76* (Washington, D.C.: American Revolution Bicentennial Administration, 1976), p. 5.

[7]Frank E. Manning, "Prelude," in *The Celebration of Society: Perspectives on Contemporary Cultural Performance,* edited by Manning (Bowling Green, Ohio: Bowling Green University Popular Press, 1983), p. x. Also see Beverly J. Stoeltje, "Festival in America," in *Handbook of American Folklore*, edited by Richard M. Dorson (Bloomington: Indiana University Press, 1983), pp. 239, 246.

[8]G. S. Metraux, "Of Feasts and Carnivals," *Cultures* (1976), 3:7.

[9]For anthropological discussions of the "reversals" that occur during celebratory activities, see the chapters in *The Celebration of Society* and in Barbara Babcock, editor, *The Reversible World* (Ithaca, New York: Cornell University Press, 1978). The classic and guiding statement of this concept is Victor Turner, "Liminal to Liminoid in Play, Flow, and Ritual: An Essay in Comparative Symbology," *Rice University Studies* (1974), 60:53-92.

[10]See Jay Anderson, *Time Machines: The World of Living History* (Nashville: American Association for State and Local History, 1984).

Preface

In 1981 the Idaho Oral History Center began a project entitled "Working Together: A Regional Approach to Community Traditions and History in Idaho." For many people involved in Idaho cultural and historical endeavors, Working Together was, during its three-year existence, a source of technical advice and support. It was my privilege to be a part of the project for those three years, working with my colleagues and friends Madeline Buckendorf and J. Sanford (Sandy) Rikoon.

Our goals were ambitious. We hoped to develop a permanent network of Idahoans working in local history and folklife projects so that people living in separate parts of the state could learn from and share the experiences of others. The idea sounds simple; but in a state as geographically, politically, and culturally diverse as Idaho, it was a difficult assignment — especially since most Idaho organizations have little money to fund visits to other locations or to hire consultants to come to them.

With funds from the National Endowment for the Humanities and the Steele-Reese Foundation, we attempted to develop this statewide network in a variety of ways. We sponsored seven major regional workshops and dozens of local workshops on topics ranging from writing local history to oral history to family history. We hosted three regional, two-day conferences on interpreting local history and culture and held a statewide conference on the diversity of local history. Perhaps the most important service offered was free consultation to groups throughout the state. These included museums, historical societies, schools, libraries, and civic organizations. We also published a regular newsletter, a series of technical leaflets, a monograph of conference papers, and this handbook.

It is no exaggeration to say that we learned as much during the project as did the people we tried to help. Wherever we went, we were surprised at the enthusiasm and innovative ideas generated for local history and folklife projects. We tried to transmit these good ideas from one group to another and saw many of them reused, adapted to fit local needs.

This handbook grew out of these experiences. Today the exchange of celebration ideas is becoming increasingly important as most states and many communities and organizations in the Northwest approach their centennials. Our travels thoughout Idaho and into Washington, Montana, and other neighboring states revealed a kind of "anniversary frenzy" appearing in the region. People who have long been active in local history view the upcoming anniversaries as a way of involving even more people in their endeavors. Those who have not been involved previously in local history see historic anniversaries as a means of developing community pride. Several groups in Idaho and the Northwest have already undertaken anniversary celebrations, and I have borrowed extensively from their experiences and ideas in this handbook. These people taught me much about planning and completing an anniversary event. I hope I have succeeded in passing on some of these good ideas to others. If the handbook succeeds in this, it will have fulfilled an important goal of Working Together.

One of our goals throughout the Working Together project has been to make accessible the work of others and not to needlessly repeat others' efforts. In planning this handbook we contacted the American Association for State and Local History and all fifty state humanities committees. We also asked the Idaho State Library and the Library of Congress to do literature searches for publications relating to anniversary celebrations. We uncovered some interesting and valuable books, articles, reports, and pamphlets, but we did not find a basic, grass-roots guide for small communities planning anniversary celebrations. We therefore believe this handbook is unique, and we hope it serves a useful purpose.

The handbook is primarily intended as a basic guide for small communities, although we hope that larger, urban areas, as well as clubs and organizations, can benefit from its information. It was planned for communities in Idaho and the western states that are approaching diamond jubilees and centennials, but we hope it will also be useful for older communities in other regions.

I have not attempted to mention every activity that could be undertaken as part of an anniversary celebration. Rather, the purpose of this handbook is to stimulate ideas. It was written on the premise that the fundamentals of all anniversary celebrations are universal. In Chapter 3 I have provided a detailed analysis of only two specific projects — planning a crafts fair and publishing local history materials. I did not include these because I believe every celebration should have a crafts fair or a publication, or because I believe these activities are more important than others mentioned. My goal was merely to offer a taste of the type of detailed and time-consuming planning and organization that is required for any successful project.

All of the specific examples in the handbook are offered as suggestions only, as each community has different needs, resources, and goals. Although there are not specific references for all examples mentioned, readers should be aware that each activity included in the handbook — whether it be fundraising, publicity, or a project idea — has been successfully completed in some small community. Not every activity is suitable for everyone, but anniversary planners should not be deterred because of a mistaken belief that they do not have the population, talent, or resources to complete a project. The three case studies in Chapter 6 bear this out. They give concrete examples of how three small, diverse communities celebrated their anniversaries. Each community example represents a significantly different ideology that resulted in different activities. Still, all three succeeded, all adhered to certain sound basics in planning and organization, and all demonstrated how anniversary celebrations can be adapted to fit local needs.

In 1973 Robert G. Hartje, anticipating the national bicentennial, wrote:

> National birthdays, like human birthdays, offer opportunities that citizens of this country should not take lightly. Birthdays symbolize more than our birth and the passing of our days. They symbolize achievement and growth, remind us of the past that shapes our present, and give hope for a productive future. The big question is not *whether* America will celebrate its national birthday; it is *how* our nation will deal with this important moment in history.[1]

The same is also true for local communities facing significant birthdays. Anniversary celebration is a part of our heritage. "There is something magic in anniversaries, those arbitrary signposts devised by mortals to chart their passage through the mystery of time," wrote Dee Brown.[2] Nearly every community will in some way mark its arbitrary signposts with celebrations. The question is not whether, but how. I hope that the residents of Idaho, the Pacific Northwest, and the United States will mark these significant mileposts with more than beard-growing contests, community parades, and the burying of time capsules. I do not suggest eliminating such festive activities, for anniversaries are meant to be fun, involving large numbers of people. But I also hope anniversary planners will be able to look back upon their hours of hard work as the source of long-lasting benefits for their communities. The primary goal of this publication is to help anniversary planners achieve those benefits.

I owe a debt to many who assisted in developing this handbook. Foremost among those I wish to acknowledge is Madeline Buckendorf, coordinator of the Idaho Oral History Center. She was the inspiration behind Working Together, was its director, chief administrator, and fundraiser. She was the first to recognize the need for a handbook such as this and provided me with many of the ideas contained herein, as well as with numerous helpful editorial comments. Sandy Rikoon not only wrote a foreword that provides a sound background for anyone contemplating an anniversary celebration, but he also read and critiqued the entire manuscript and offered valuable suggestions.

Jerry Glenn, librarian at Ricks College in Rexburg; Dean May, of the Department of History at the University of Utah; Mary Reed, director of the Latah County Historical Society in Moscow; Nancy Renk, independent historian from Sandpoint; and David Stratton, then chairman of the Department of History at Washington State University, all read the manuscript and offered criticism and advice. Kathleen Probasco of Moscow labored many hours deciphering my handwriting prior to completing three typed drafts. Virginia Ricketts, of the Jerome County Historical Society, and Bill Lang, editor of *Montana: The*

Magazine of Western History, evaluated the handbook for the Association for the Humanities in Idaho.

Louis Clements, Rexburg; Archie Hulsizer, Wallace; Virginia Ricketts, Jerome; and Lorene Thurston, Caldwell, all provided helpful information about their community celebrations. Marty Peterson, now administrator of the Idaho Division of Financial Management but at the time director of the Association of Idaho Cities, was one of the first to recognize a need for such a handbook and approached Working Together as the logical organization to write it.

In 1983 Madeline and I met in Coeur d'Alene with a group of north Idaho people long associated with regional history and folklife projects to discuss ideas for the handbook. Those present, who offered many suggestions and much encouragement, included Sherry Boswell, Lorelea Hudson, Nancy Luebbert, Dave Osterberg, Mary Reed, and Nancy Renk. The Working Together project advisory council likewise offered advice throughout the planning stages. Members of the council were Judy Austin, Charles Bolles, Jackie Day, Tom Green, Tom Rybus, Steve Siporin, Ann Swanson, Ken Swanson, and Don Watts.

Finally, acknowledgement is due the Association for the Humanities in Idaho, the National Endowment for the Humanities, and the Steele-Reese Foundation. These institutions supported Working Together throughout the project. Their interest in and support of local history is commendable. We thank them for their confidence in us and hope they are pleased with this publication.

Pullman, Washington
May 1985

NOTES

[1]Robert G. Hartje, *Bicentennial USA: Pathways to Celebration* (Nashville: American Association for State and Local History, 1973), p. 11.

[2]Dee Brown, *The Year of the Century: 1876* (New York: Charles Scribner's Sons, 1966), p. 1.

1

Project Organization

An anniversary celebration will only be as successful as the planning that precedes it. Dates and themes must be selected, committees chosen, goals set, activities planned, deadlines met, and legal requirements adhered to. Organizers of anniversary celebrations must be hard-working individuals willing to meet often, over a long period of time.

FIRST STEPS: BEGIN EARLY, SELECT COMMITTEES

The most common mistake made by anniversary groups is to begin planning too late. As Becky Hart, a key coordinator of the Preston, Idaho, centennial celebration of 1983, stated, "If I were to do another centennial celebration, I would start serious plans a year or two in advance." The size of the celebration and the types of projects envisioned will dictate the amount of lead time necessary to properly organize the festivities. If only a few short-term projects are anticipated — a parade or a crafts festival, for example — perhaps a year of planning will be ample. If numerous projects are to be attempted, including long-term ones such as the writing of a local history book or the organization of a museum, three to four years of planning, research, and other tasks might be necessary. For example, Utah will celebrate its centennial in 1996 and a committee began planning for it in 1982. Indeed, it is hard to imagine a celebration of any sort succeeding with less than a year of preliminary planning.[1]

It is also hard to imagine a successful anniversary celebration that was not planned by a committee. Choosing a central planning committee requires careful thought. Its size will vary according to the size of the community and the number and types of projects to be undertaken. There is no ideal size for such a committee. Most people who have been through an anniversary celebration agree, however, that ten to twelve people is about the maximum size for top efficiency. Larger committees can be cumbersome and ineffective because of erratic attendance, divisive debate, and difficulty in reaching consensus. It is important that the committee represent a diversity of community interests, but obviously not every interest group can have a representative on the central com-

1

mittee and its members should be seen as representing the whole community
rather than only one segment. As explained later, there are ways of ensuring
representation without burdening the planning committee with too many
members. A dynamic chairperson is also essential to keep plans moving on
schedule. It is important that there not be two or more committees working
on separate celebrations of the same anniversary without coordination. "Nothing
could be more disastrous than to have two competing groups trying to plan
a centennial," noted Louis Clements, chairman of the Rexburg, Idaho, centennial committee.[2]

At some point in early discussions about planning for an anniversary, someone
will mention the possibility of hiring a person or firm to undertake planning
for the festivities. The idea of leaving all of the headaches and details to someone else is an attractive one, and occasionally some communities do turn to
such outside help and express satisfaction afterward. As a general rule, however,
the temptation for small communities to hire professional organizers — especially those from outside the local area — should be resisted. The thirty-year-old
advice of Raymond Sivesind, who wrote *How to Organize a Centennial Celebration,* is still timely: "With effective local leadership, there should be no need
for engaging commercial companies which all too often produce substantially
the same stereotyped celebration wherever they go with injection of a few local
names and events to give the production a semblance of local atmosphere."
Competent consultants can greatly assist a local community, especially in the
early planning stages. But the nuts and bolts of organizational details are usually
best accomplished by local volunteers working on their own celebration.[3]

Among those who should obviously be considered for committee membership are professional historians, anthropologists, folklorists, and museum personnel, especially if they have experience working with local groups. Most
small western communities will not have such resident professionals, but it may
be well to ask some from outside the area to work with the planning committee. State historical societies and state humanities committees can usually refer
anniversary planners to nearby professionals who have worked on similar
projects in the past.

Beyond these professionals, the planning committee might include elected
officials and community leaders as well as members of service clubs, the
chamber of commerce, women's clubs, and church groups. Every segment of
a community should be involved if the celebration is to be successful. Be sure
to contact representatives of special-interest groups such as the elderly, labor
unions, ethnic groups, and disabled persons. And do not overlook the local
historical society. Staff and volunteers at these organizations work daily on ways
to commemorate the past and can offer the central committee years of experience
at solving many of the very problems the anniversary planners will face.

Professional historians, folklorists, and museum staff can help the committee from its earliest planning stages through the completion of the celebration. (Idaho State Historical Society)

Even the smallest towns are rich in highly qualified personnel who can assist in planning anniversary celebrations. The local newspaper editor can describe how to write news releases; the fine-arts teacher (or his students) can design logos and posters; a local business owner can recommend accounting procedures; a moving company can provide needed transportation vehicles; an attorney can assist with legal advice. While it is at times necessary to bring outside consultants into your community to plan specific details, look first at home to see if there is someone with similar expertise who can help. Utilizing local resources will not only be less expensive but also encourage a broader base of participation in the celebration.

While the central planning committee obviously needs hardworking members, some of the most dedicated, highly skilled residents of a community have little "name appeal." Thus many committees also include people whose names are well recognized in the region, but who might not have the time or inclination to work actively on the celebration. Included among such individuals may be the town mayor, school superintendent, state senator, newspaper publisher, owner of the largest business, and other local dignitaries.

The usefulness of having prestigious names associated with the anniversary celebration should not be underestimated. These people can unlock publicity and fundraising doors that might be permanently closed to a hardworking but unknown central committee. These local celebrities may well lend more than just their names to your celebration. In all likelihood, however, they will be too busy to oversee minute details or attend numerous meetings. Rather than burdening the central planning committee with too many inactive members, it is often better to have a separate steering or advisory committee of well-known local and regional personalities. This committee should be kept well informed of celebration plans and should also be expected to provide some assistance. It should not, however, be expected to undertake all of the detailed planning necessary for a successful event. That is the task of the central committee.

While a committee that has representatives from every segment of a community can be too unwieldy to function properly, certainly all interested groups should be informed of plans and invited to comment upon proposed activities. There are several ways in which community opinions can be obtained. One of the most effective methods is to hold a town meeting and invite the public and specific organizations to present ideas and proposals. The community is more likely to support plans if its residents feel they have had an opportunity to contribute to them. Another effective method, particularly if you hope to reach a wide variety of groups, is to have a series of workshops with each targeted group, seeking comment and advice. Still another way is to form a large advisory committee to stimulate ideas. Such a committee will normally be too large to actually plan activities, but brainstorming sessions in large advisory committees with many segments of a community represented can be an outstanding way of gauging community sentiment.

Another way to involve many segments of the community is to utilize groups already functioning in your area, developing a network of existing organizations rather than starting everything anew. "Plan on using your town's existing organized groups rather than a whole series of small new committees with specific tasks," stated an organizer of the Erie County, New York, sesquicentennial celebration of 1971. "Existing groups already know what each of their members [is] capable of contributing, thus the work can begin right away."[4]

These established organizations can also provide subcommittees to the central planning committee. For example, local singing groups may be in charge of musical entertainment, while the school speech class can produce dramatic presentations. Even if existing groups are not used in this manner, subcommittees should be formed to keep plans progressing. In this way the central committee can serve as the overall planning and administering body while delegating details to various subgroups. The number of subcommittees and their assignments will vary with each celebration, but among the subcommittees you will want to consider are:

— physical arrangements, to check on building regulations, lighting, sound, street closures, garbage disposal, set-up, and clean-up;

— publicity, to handle contacts with newspapers, radio, and television, and to distribute posters, flyers, and other publicity materials;

— cultural activities, to stimulate artistic and creative activities in local areas of interest such as handcrafts, literature, music, and photography;

— educational activities, to encourage school participation in the celebration;

—religious activities, to encourage participation by local churches and synagogues;

— tourist promotion, to encourage area motels, restaurants, the chamber of commerce, and regional tourism commissions to feature details about the celebration;

— fundraising, to solicit revenue both before and during the celebration;

— hospitality, to provide hosts and hostesses for events and to make sure everyone who helps is adequately thanked.

Among the first tasks of the central committee will be the assigning of specific chores, including subcommittee tasks; scheduling regular meeting times; opening a bank account; and arranging for a headquarters, or at the least a telephone number and mailing address where community questions can be directed. This can be the address and number of a committee member if that person does not mind interruptions, but if a large celebration is planned it is best to have a post office box and a headquarters with a telephone — perhaps an office space donated by a local business. Such a headquarters can also provide valuable public exposure for your celebration. When Caldwell, Idaho, celebrated its centennial in 1983, the project coordinator was provided free office space first in the public library and later in city hall. This highly visible space gave the celebration considerable exposure and, according to centennial organizer Lorene Thurston, was "one of the very, very important aspects of the whole celebration."[5]

GOALSETTING, ESTABLISHING A TIMETABLE, AND SCHEDULING ACTIVITIES

It will be the task of the central committee not only to select subcommittees, but also to establish goals and a timetable for the celebration. In fact, these should be among the first of the committee's activities. Establishing the overall goals of the celebration is a significant activity, for they will dictate the types of projects to be undertaken. For example, if the chief goal of the celebration is to "involve most of the members of the community," this might be accomplished with a parade and a fair. However, if the goals are loftier, such as to "instill a deeper knowledge of local history in the people of the area," a completely different set of projects might be planned, such as the development of a traveling exhibit or school curriculum packages.

Specific goals, tied to specific deadlines, are essential to the success of any project. Goals should be reasonable and attainable. Having specific objectives will enable you to see the results of your work. Volunteers can see what has been accomplished and feel rewarded. Shared objectives provide participants with something solid to work toward. If specific goals are not established at the outset, enthusiasm will likely wane as the planning committee flounders in a myriad of details, unable to reward its members for accomplishing any agreed-upon objectives.

The central committee is likely to establish several goals and choose a variety of long-term and short-term projects to meet them. The number of activities that can successfully be pursued depends upon the number of people serving on the central committee and the subcommittees, the amount of time they have to devote to the celebration, their skill levels, and the amount of money they have to work with. Everyone who has been through an anniversary celebration before, however, seems to agree with Becky Hart that it is better "not to be overly ambitious." Instead, choose "a few quality projects over many."[6]

It is best not to focus entirely upon the past. The New Jersey Tercentenary Commission stated that the philosophy of its celebration should "not be a 'backward-looking' spirit . . . rather, the approach should be from the past to the present — and thence to the future." Celebrating the Massachusetts Bay Tercentenary in the depths of the Great Depression, that state, too, found it desirable to have a celebration that reflected on the past while it "inspire[d] confidence for the future." History should be more than a glorification of pioneer roots. The primary purpose of history is to help us learn how we have arrived at where we are, and consequently to provide a foundation upon which to plan for the future. Anniversary celebrations provide a unique opportunity to learn from the past while planning for the future, because so many people who normally show little or no interest in an area's history will participate in a celebration.[7]

Selecting project activities should also be done with care, but too often groups spend so much time selecting activities they do not allow enough time to implement them. This is another good reason to begin planning early; as the North Carolina Confederate Centennial Commission *Guide* stated: "The important thing is to utilize your time working on a program rather than selecting it."[8]

The most successful celebrations are those with enough diversity to involve large numbers of people. Project activities should have both short-term and long-term impact. Too often when we attend anniversary celebrations we are presented only with gala pageantry during which members of a community sport new beards, dress up in old-time clothes, have a parade, bury a time capsule, and then promptly forget about their heritage until another significant anniversary arrives. There is a place for pageantry in our celebrations, and those who try to take all the fun and festivity out of an anniversary will find themselves laboring long hours for a very small audience. But celebrations can be both enjoyable and valuable, and the central committee should arrange for short-term projects like contests and concerts as well as long-term activities that contribute to the preservation and interpretation of the community's history, such as gathering historic photographs and conducting oral history interviews.

The central committee will want to time the various celebration activities carefully. For example, a college town should not plan all of its activities for the summer when students are away. An agricultural community will not want to have its main activities occur during harvest season. And almost every community should avoid conflict with local school sports, such as a regional or state tournament. Similarly, potential conflicts with well-established annual events should be noted. Many town chambers of commerce maintain community calendars and these should be consulted, as should area schools. While you will not want to compete with such established activities as a county fair or an annual crafts show, it is entirely possible these can become a part of the anniversary celebration merely by asking the organizers of the events to incorporate an anniversary theme into their plans. Or the central committee might want to plan its major activities around an event like a county fair when a good crowd will be guaranteed.

While an anniversary celebration should not compete with a well-established event, it is possible to incorporate an anniversary theme into an annual activity such as a county fair. That is what Jerome did during its Diamond Jubilee. (Jerome County Historical Society)

SELECTING A CELEBRATORY DATE AND THEME

Another early task of any central planning committee will be to select a date to celebrate. In some cases selecting a date or year of celebration is quite simple. If the first sermon of a local church was preached in 1887, then the most logical time to celebrate the church's centennial would be 1987. In many cases, however, selecting the "arbitrary signpost" upon which to peg a celebration is not so straightforward. For example, many communities are "towns" long before they are incorporated as such. Moscow, Idaho, was first settled in 1871 and received a post office in 1876. But it was not incorporated until 1887, when it had a population of over 1,000. Which date should it select to celebrate? One answer to the question might be to celebrate all the dates. That is what British Columbia did when it had a difficult time selecting the most suitable centennial to recognize. Thus, in 1958 it celebrated the 100th anniversary of the founding of the mainland Colony of British Columbia; in 1967 it celebrated national confederation along with the rest of Canada's provinces; and in 1971 it commemorated the province's entry into confederation with Canada.

Most small communities, however, do not have the financial or volunteer resources to undertake a number of consecutive, successful celebrations, so establishing a celebratory date becomes an important task. One of the first things groups considering such a celebration can do is research and outline a brief chronological history of their community so that a number of dates can be discussed. Keep in mind that almost any date selected for celebration will be arbitrary, for few communities can be said to have a single date when they suddenly "began." The success of your celebration will be contingent upon proper organization, not the selection of a particular date. Nonetheless, choosing a "significant" date — usually from a list of several that could well qualify — will help your celebration succeed. Most people like to have their pasts neatly aligned into decades and centuries, and you will find some people, including the press, much more willing to support your efforts if a significant date has been selected.

The central committee will need to establish a theme for the celebration. A catchy theme, like a significant date, can do wonders for generating interest. Caldwell, Idaho, chose "100 Years of Action ... Growth ... and Progress ... That's Caldwell!" as its theme, while the Jerome, Idaho, theme was simply "The North Side ... A Cause for Pride." The state of Washington has selected "Celebrate! '89" for its centennial theme, while Alaska selected "North to the Future" for its 1964 centennial slogan. In each case the theme is catchy and easy to remember and repeat, and it conveys in a few words the general ideals of the central planning committee. A good theme can establish an instant identity for the celebration. An official logo or symbol can evolve from the theme, and such a device can greatly aid in publicity.

SEEKING OFFICIAL RECOGNITION AND MEETING LEGAL REQUIREMENTS

Another organizational activity of the planning committee should be to have the mayor, city council, county commissioners or some other such official body pass a resolution or proclamation recognizing the committee as the official anniversary planning group and recognizing its plans as the official celebratory activities. If the committee is going to establish a logo, slogan, or symbol, an official resolution can also be passed prohibiting other groups and businesses from using these symbols without permission (and perhaps for a fee). Such official recognition lends prestige to a celebration and can help in promoting interest, generating publicity, and raising funds.

Finally, the central planning committee will need to make sure its celebration plans meet legal requirements. For this purpose, it is helpful to have an attorney on the planning committee. One of the first things the lawyer should do is complete the necessary paperwork required for the anniversary committee to obtain nonprofit, tax-exempt status. Obtaining nonprofit status from the state and tax-exempt status from the state and Internal Revenue Service can be time-consuming, so such efforts must begin early. As an alternative, the committee may want to work through an organization that already has such status, such as a local historical society, library, or governmental agency. In either case, being nonprofit and tax-exempt can greatly assist fundraising efforts as businesses, individuals, and foundations can then make tax-deductible contributions to the anniversary celebration.

There are usually many other legal ramifications to consider in any celebration, and the committee's attorney should be consulted frequently during the early planning stages. For example, parade permits may be required; restrooms can be mandated if a large crowd is to gather at a certain location for a period of time; taxes can be required on sales of certain items even if tax-exempt status has been received; food vending may be subject to certain regulations; alcohol may not be allowed in certain places; and so forth.

Each anniversary celebration is unique and each central committee will soon find that it has many diverse organizational plans to develop. The primary rule is to meet early and often. This chapter and the checklist that follows offer guidance for some of the major organizational tasks of any celebration. In addition to these, the committee will identify a myriad of important details as its plans progress.

PROJECT ORGANIZATION CHECKLIST

☐ Begin planning early
☐ Select committees
   ☐ Central planning committee
   ☐ Blue-ribbon advisory committee
   ☐ Subcommittees
☐ Solicit community opinions on the celebration, through such means as town meetings and workshops
☐ Develop a network with existing organizations, clubs, and groups
☐ Establish celebration goals and objectives
   ☐ Plan short-term and long-term activities to meet the goals
☐ Develop a timetable of deadlines
☐ Establish a headquarters, or mailing address, and telephone number
☐ Select dates for undertaking various activities
☐ Select a date to celebrate
   ☐ Develop a local chronology of dates that could serve as significant anniversary dates
☐ Select an anniversary theme
   ☐ Develop a logo or symbol evolving from the theme
☐ Solicit official recognition for the anniversary celebration
☐ Meet all legal requirements
   ☐ Establish nonprofit, tax-exempt status
   ☐ Be aware of local ordinances that might affect celebratory plans

NOTES

[1]The quotation is from Madeline Buckendorf, "Centennials and Diamond Jubilees: Some Project Examples," *Working Together Newsletter* (Idaho State Historical Society) (Fall 1982), p. 2.

[2]Louis J. Clements, "So You Are Going to Plan a Centennial Celebration," *Snake River Echoes, Quarterly Journal of the Upper Snake River Valley Historical Society* (1983), 12/1:24.

[3]Raymond S. Sivesind, *How to Organize a Centennial Celebration*, Bulletin No. 100 (Madison: State Historical Society of Wisconsin, 1956), p. 4.

[4]Walter S. Dunn, Jr., *Local Historical Celebrations*, Information Sheet No. 20 (Manlius, N.Y.: Regional Conference of Historical Agencies, [1975?]), p. 1.

[5]Lorene Thurston, Caldwell Historic Preservation Commission, interview with Madeline Buckendorf, Caldwell, Idaho, December 17, 1984.

[6]Buckendorf, "Centennials and Diamond Jubilees," p. 3.

[7]The quotations are from *The New Jersey Tercentenary, 1664-1964* (Trenton: New Jersey Tercentenary Commission, 1966), p. 8, and *Celebrating a 300th Anniversary* (Boston: Tercentenary Conference of City & Town Committees, 1931), p. 17.

[8]*Centennial Guide for Local Committees* (Raleigh: North Carolina Confederate Centennial Commission, 1960), p. 4.

2

Fundraising

Fundraising is more an art than a science. Both the ability to raise money and the sources of that money vary widely from community to community and state to state. The basic generalization to keep in mind is that "results in fund raising are achieved when the right person asks the right prospect for the right amount, for the right reason, at the right time."[1]

SOME FUNDRAISING FUNDAMENTALS

Good fundraising follows good programming

This is the most important rule of any fundraising activity, but unfortunately it is also the most overlooked. In their effort to raise money for various projects, people often lose sight of the fact that fundraising in and of itself is not a goal—it is merely a means of reaching a goal. The goal of the anniversary planning committee should be to have a successful celebration, and some money will be needed in order to succeed. Therefore, fundraising is necessary. However, individuals, businesses, organizations, and granting agencies will support your efforts only if they are assured that you have sound ideas for projects and the ability to carry them out successfully. Fundraising is very competitive, with many worthwhile organizations seeking shares of a limited pool of money. Therefore, the most important priority of the anniversary committee should be to plan good programs. Only then should funds be sought to finance the projects envisioned. Do not first attempt to raise money and then try to figure out what projects you can undertake with the funds available.

People give in order to get

There is a misconception that charitable donors give to a cause simply because it is worthy. Some people do this, but the majority of donors want to receive something in return for their contribution. This does not mean the anniversary committee has to give gifts to all donors, although some organizations find this a useful way to recruit contributions. Rather, donors must be made to feel they are investing in something they care about. You should also keep in mind that most people want to contribute to healthy organizations. Very little successful fundraising is undertaken out of dire need. You must demonstrate that your anniversary committee is a vital organization prepared to do outstanding work. Make your case from a position of strength, not weakness.

Investigate professional fundraisers before paying for their services

There are many individuals and professional fundraising firms who are eager to provide you with advice or help you raise money — for a fee. Sometimes their services are helpful, but there is little a professional fundraiser can tell you that you cannot learn yourself through study and asking questions. Remember that successful fundraising requires a knowledge of your particular area and needs. It is unlikely that an outside fundraiser will have the depth of knowledge required to be as successful as dedicated local individuals. This is not to say that hiring professional fundraisers is bad policy. However, you should enter into a contract only after thorough study. If you decide that a professional fundraiser would be advantageous, find out as much as you can about him or her. Has he raised money for celebratory activities in the past? Has he specifically raised money for historical anniversaries? Has he worked in small towns, or is his experience limited to areas like Seattle or San Francisco?

Know your area

Most funds for local celebrations will come from the local area. Study your area for its funding potential. What organizations and projects have received community support in the past? Why have some succeeded and others failed? What types of appeals did the successful groups make? How were their fundraising drives organized? Begin keeping files on local businesses and civic clubs by watching the newspapers and asking friends about them. Do they make contributions to local groups? If so, how large are the contributions? Will businesses give money at any time of the year, or is a year-end, pre-tax-deadline period the best time to approach them? Will civic clubs sponsor fundraisers for specific causes? Remember, too, that by far the major source of all charitable contributions in the United States is donations by individuals. Gather membership lists of various organizations in your area. Watch the newspapers and again consult friends to see which individuals have made donations in the past. Above all, remember that your area might be different from other towns where successful fundraisers have taken place. Merely because you have heard of an activity succeeding in some other location does not mean it will succeed in your town. A tour of gardens might work in California, but in Idaho a tractor-pulling competition might raise more money.

Begin fundraising on a local level, expanding to the state, regional, and national levels only if needed

While most funds will come from the local area, some communities may require additional money to undertake their projects. These funds may come in the form of a corporate contribution, a grant from a governmental agency or foundation, or a gift from a regional tourism commission. Competition for outside funding is even more competitive than local fundraising, and most outside sources will check to see that the committee requesting aid has a good track record in managing funds and has local support. You will be much more successful in approaching state, regional, or national funding sources if you can show that you have already raised a considerable amount of local money — and spent it prudently — and that you have a broad base of support from many local individuals, groups, and businesses. Sometimes the number of contributors is almost as important as the amount of money they give. If you live in a depressed area and your average contribution is only $5, but several hundred individuals have contributed, make this into an asset rather than a liability. Explain to outside funding sources that your cause has broad grassroots support, but that local people cannot pay for all of the good ideas you have and therefore additional, outside assistance is required.

Have a diversity of fundraising activities

It is generally unreasonable to expect that you will get all of the money you need from one source. Proceeds will more than likely come from a variety of places — grants, business donations, individual contributions, sales, and so forth. As any good business person knows, revenue should be diversified. If you rely too heavily on a single source, your entire celebration can be placed in jeopardy if, for some reason, that source is unable to continue making donations or cannot make the amount pledged or anticipated. Make it possible for everyone to contribute. A $1,000 business donation will help you more than a $1 raffle ticket sale; but if you sell a thousand raffle tickets, they will not only provide a sizable amount of money but also serve as publicity because you have involved many people who want to support your efforts but cannot afford to give large amounts.

Become familiar with fundraising literature

As the necessity and competitiveness of fundraising have increased, so has the number of books written about the subject. There are books on every aspect of the topic from how to organize bake sales to how to write major grants. Many of these contain helpful hints, and you should become familiar with some of the better ones before embarking on a fundraising campaign: there is no sense in "re-inventing the wheel." The bibliography in this handbook will direct you to some of the better fundraising guides.

Start fundraising early

Fundraising will be one of the most challenging tasks faced by the anniversary planning committee. Raising even modest amounts of money in small communities can take a considerable amount of time since successful fundraising events cannot be thrown together overnight. If you plan to write grants, allow for the fact that this too is exceedingly time-consuming. There are also good times and bad times of the year to raise money. For example, individuals tend not to make large contributions in March and April when they are filling out income-tax forms, but are more likely to give in November and December when they are looking for year-end charitable contributions. Most granting agencies have deadlines you must meet, and sometimes these come only once a year. If you have not planned well enough and miss a deadline, your whole project can be delayed. A bake sale in your area might not be successful around Christmas because of too much competition but could go over well in the summer. Conversely, a rummage sale might face too much competition from garage sales in the summer but might, because of the unusual timing, do very well in the winter. You must start your planning early to evaluate all possible eventualities; fundraising of any type is time-consuming, and it is a waste of time to organize a fundraiser or write a grant only to realize later that it was unsuccessful because it was mistimed.

Specific projects are easier to raise money for than are ongoing activities

Fundraisers for museums have known for years that it is much easier to raise money to build a new museum building than for paying the utility bills or hiring staff once the building is constructed. People — including most granting agencies — like to give to something visible with a definite date of completion. Therefore, you might have difficulty raising money if you just ask for donations "for our anniversary celebration." People want to know more specifically what they are giving money to. You will have better luck if you break your celebration into components and seek funding on a project-by-project basis. Thus businesses might support a parade because it will bring people downtown; the local Grange might fund an exhibit on the history of agriculture in the area; and the senior-citizens club might help pay for an oral history project.

Personal contact is vital

Too often organizations are hoodwinked into believing that all they need is a fancy package to make their fundraising efforts successful. They produce a brochure explaining why they need money, mail these out to every business in town, and then sit back waiting for the money to come in. Unfortunately, in most cases the money simply does not arrive. Campaigns are not won on the strength of packaging. They are won by hard work and personal contact. While there is something to be said for looking professional and packaging a funding request handsomely, there is a fine line between looking professional and looking Madison Avenue slick — and most residents of small communities are less than eager to contribute to something they think is too slick. Beyond this, however, an impersonal brochure, no matter how nicely designed, will never be as successful as personal contact. The American Cancer Society raises millions of dollars each year by going door to door in towns throughout the country. Girl Scouts successfully raise money by selling cookies the same way. Neither group would be nearly as successful if it merely had a passive campaign of mailing out requests for donations. People are much more likely to give if they are approached personally, and the same goes for businesses, service clubs, and other organizations. Find people who know business owners or individuals able to make substantial contributions and ask them to go with you to contact those people. Too many fundraisers shy away from such contact because they feel it is an imposition. Actually, if handled properly by setting up appointments beforehand, such meetings can be fruitful for all involved. At the very least you will have informed one more person of the upcoming celebration. And your chances of receiving support from that person are much greater than if you had only sent him a brochure in the mail.

Know your source before asking for money

Generic requests generally do not work, and the shotgun approach is less successful than a rifle approach. This is especially true of grant-writing: it is not worth your time writing grant proposals if you do not first research the granting agency to determine the types of projects it will fund and the kinds of proposals it wants to receive. Too many people think they can write one grant proposal and then simply copy it and mail it off to dozens of foundations or government granting agencies. Such a strategy rarely works. Even on a local level, research will be rewarded. If a local person is a teetotaler, for example, it would be embarrassing to ask him to an exclusive wine-tasting party.

Fundraising can include items other than money

People too often feel that fundraising refers only to raising money. In-kind contributions should also be sought. A lumber yard might find it easier to donate $100 worth of lumber than to write a $100 check to your committee. A local business might be able to provide you with a few hours of free secretarial time each week. The newspaper might provide free advertising space. A farmer might allow you to use his property to set up a billboard. A restaurant might cater a fundraising meal. An office machine business might loan you a typewriter or filing cabinet. Use your imagination and seek in-kind contributions just as diligently as you solicit money. It is entirely possible these contributions will amount to more in the long run than your cash donations.

Contributors must be acknowledged

There is no quicker way to dampen community enthusiasm for a celebration than to let donations of time, money, or materials go unacknowledged. Each donation should be acknowledged as quickly as possible. It is preferable to do this in writing, demonstrating that you care enough about the contribution to take the time to write. Donors will not become loyal friends of your anniversary planning committee if they think you are interested only in money. In addition to a written thank-you, you might want to take additional steps to acknowledge contributions, such as:

— having a reception for donors;
— having a special "club" for donors who contribute over a certain amount, such as a "Centennial Club" for contributions of $100 or more for a centennial celebration;
— publishing donors' names in your reports, event programs, brochures, or newsletters;
— providing media publicity for outstanding gifts, if the donors approve of this idea.

FUNDRAISING FOR AN ANNIVERSARY CELEBRATION

Anniversary celebrations have traditionally provided the impetus for successful fundraising. The centennial celebration of 1876 in Philadelphia attracted eight million paying customers, despite the fact that before the event many people doubted it would succeed because "business was bad everywhere, banks were failing in many cities, wages were down to one dollar a day for factory workers, desperate farmers in the Midwest were burning corn for fuel." The Massachusetts Bay Tercentenary also brought revenue into that state despite being held in 1930, a time when other states were suffering badly. The British Columbia Centennial of 1959 saw a dramatic increase in tourist revenue in a year when neighboring states and provinces suffered declines.[2]

It is likely your committee will want to raise money both before and during the celebration. No one can put together a celebration for nothing, so some money must be sought in advance. You might want to use money raised during the event itself to pay off the final bills, or you may want to use it for one of the celebration's long-term projects, such as the publication of a local history book or development of a community museum. It is impossible to detail all fundraising possibilities in a handbook of this type. Again, you are encouraged to read some of the available fundraising literature and to speak to others in your community who have raised money. What follows are a few suggestions for local, state, and national fundraising that may stimulate further ideas.

LOCAL FUNDRAISING

As stated before, the majority of funds for most community celebrations will come from the local area. The possibilities here are also the broadest. Bake sales, door-to-door campaigns, rummage sales, auctions, membership drives, souvenir sales, food fairs, homes tours, concerts, dances, raffles, and many more methods are possible. For suggestions on grassroots fundraising ideas, refer to some of the books listed in the bibliography.

In addition to "generic" grassroots fundraisers like those above, many communities have found that anniversary celebrations can stimulate unique and successful fundraising events. Many of the project activities discussed in the next chapter, for example, can double as fundraisers for anniversary celebrations. The Charleston, South Carolina, Tricentennial Committee raised $230,000 in eleven months prior to its celebration by selling special coins, pictorial histories, and a phonograph record, and it used the money to finance various activities. In fact, anniversary celebrations are an excellent time to produce special coins or medallions, which are always popular with collectors. The Wallace, Idaho, centennial committee had a very successful medallion sale for that town's celebration. If properly advertised, these medallions can even be sold outside the local area. There is, of course, a gamble in producing medallions or other souvenirs as they cost money, so get a feel for your area to determine if their sale would be successful before launching into such a campaign. Talk to collectors and non-collectors alike to see if they would be willing to purchase such items, and how much they would be willing to pay.[3]

Historical publications are one of the most popular and successful fundraising activities for anniversary celebrations. People seem to eagerly await new local histories during major anniversaries, and sales then are traditionally greater than is normally expected for local historical books. You can help create a market by letting it be known in advance that a new local history will be published. Pre-publication sales, perhaps at a discount, are another way of generating enthusiasm and anticipation in the community. Your efforts should be especially successful if no local history book has been published in a number of years.

Most communities write new histories to commemorate their anniversaries, but the republishing of out-of-print local titles can also be very successful. A

Above: *The Idaho territorial centennial medal was a major memento and fundraiser for the 1963 celebration.* Below: *The Caldwell, Idaho, centennial calendar provided an abundance of interesting historical material and sold briskly. (Both, Idaho State Historical Society)*

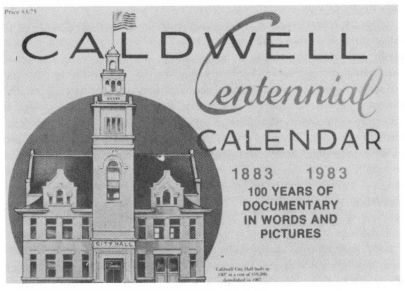

small town in New Jersey raised enough money through the republication of an 1853 town map to restore a building for a community museum during the state Tercentenary celebration. Cookbooks and calendars are also popular items. Caldwell, Idaho, published a very popular calendar as part of its centennial celebration in 1983. Each date recounted some vignette of Caldwell history and the calendar was illustrated with historic photographs. Sales were so brisk that profits were used to defray expenses involved in hiring a centennial coordinator who then spearheaded many celebration activities. You should keep in mind, however, that publication costs are constantly rising, and it is getting more difficult to make money on publications with small printings of 2,000 copies or less. Nonetheless, this can still be a profitable venture if your committee shops around for the best printing costs and properly markets the item. It is also possible to defray some of the costs by having the publication subsidized by businesses or funding agencies, or by receiving a discount from the printer. The Latah County Historical Society, which had previously published nearly twenty books on the history of that Idaho county, successfully raised enough money to hire an author to write a history celebrating the 80th anniversary of Potlatch, Idaho, and to publish the manuscript in the form of a handsome book. It raised the money primarily by soliciting contributions of $50 or more from Potlatch businesses and past and present residents of the town. There are several other local historical societies in the Northwest that have experience in publishing local history books. Contact these groups to learn from their experiences.

Souvenirs of various types are extremely popular. People buy these as keepsakes of the anniversary celebration and frequently they are handed down as family heirlooms. In addition to raising money, they also serve as a means of publicizing the celebration. Souvenirs that have been successful in other anniversary celebrations include plates, decals, posters, bumper stickers, jewelry, balloons, glasses, decanters, T-shirts, caps, towels, jackets, and innumerable miniature collectibles. These are normally not as expensive to produce as medallions or publications, but they do represent an up-front investment and therefore a gamble. Again, know your market before embarking on the production of a line of souvenirs. You should try to have souvenirs in several price ranges so that they will be within the means of all economic segments of the population. You may want to protect your celebration logo or slogan, if you have one, so that only the anniversary committee will be able to market souvenirs with the logo/slogan on them.

Local governmental agencies, such as the city council or county commission, may be willing to earmark some funds to be utilized specifically for an anniversary celebration. The Caldwell, Idaho, centennial celebration, for example, was partially funded with city revenue-sharing money. The chamber of commerce or business organizations should also be approached, because celebrations always bring tourists and business into a community. The Jerome, Idaho, diamond-jubilee celebration was successful primarily because it had the support of the Jerome Chamber of Commerce. A local bank may be willing to offer a special low-interest loan for the celebration if you can use pledges or donations as collateral. Finally, do not forget to contact your local historical society. While it will probably not be able to provide you with money (although sometimes even this is possible), it is a great source of in-kind contributions. Most have buildings that can be used, archives that can be researched, and members with a wealth of knowledge about the history of your area. It is unfortunate that too many anniversaries are celebrated without making the local historical society a key component of the event.

STATE FUNDRAISING

Once you leave the local area, fundraising becomes increasingly competitive. However, some communities will want to incorporate celebratory ideas that are simply not affordable using only local money. If that is the case, do not be afraid to seek money from state or national funding sources. These agencies appreciate good ideas, and there is no reason why your project cannot be as good — or as fundable — as another community's. A considerable amount of money and expertise is available on the state level to assist in your fundraising efforts. Appendices A and B at the back of this handbook provide addresses for several state and federal agencies that can offer funding or other services to help with local anniversary celebrations.

With the exception of Oregon — which celebrated in 1959 — every Northwest state will have its state centennial in the next few years: Montana, Washington, and the Dakotas in 1989; Idaho and Wyoming in 1990. Some of these states have already formed state centennial commissions and the others will likely follow. It is also likely that some states will offer matching grants to communities to assist in local celebrations. Even if grants are not available, you should be aware of the services offered by the state centennial commission. It may be able to provide you with free consultation services, or send you newsletters or other helpful publications that will assist in your celebration plans. David Stratton, a member of the Washington State Centennial Commission, advises that all local anniversary committees "should find out about their state centennial bodies early and keep up with their development and programs."[4]

Each state has a humanities and an arts commission. These are the state-based affiliates of the National Endowment for the Humanities and the National Endowment for the Arts respectively. Funds are provided to them by the National Endowments, as well as by individuals, businesses, and foundations, and these monies are dispersed in the form of matching grants in a wide

22

range of areas. These commissions have guidelines that will help you determine if they are able to finance projects you have planned. Humanities committees, for example, can provide grants for exhibits, slide shows, historic walking tours, radio broadcasts, presentations of historical plays, outside consultants, workshops, and so forth. Arts committees can provide grants for musical groups to perform at functions, artists in schools, folk-arts demonstrations, and many other activities.

Although northwestern states are headquarters to fewer foundations than are their eastern counterparts, each state has at least some foundations that award grants in their home areas. It is essential that you carefully research foundations before submitting a grant application. Most have specific guidelines about what they will and will not fund. Some, for example, fund only medical research, while others fund only fine-arts organizations and some give money only for scholarships. Do not waste time writing a grant proposal until you are sure the foundation gives grants in your areas of interest. Each state has a Foundation Center Library that can provide you with information not only about foundations in your state but about those in other areas as well. In addi-

State centennial commissions can offer advice on local celebrations and can keep all residents informed of anniversary activities in various parts of the state. (Idaho State Historical Society)

Washington Centennial Commission, Vol. 3, No. 1, March/April 1986

Jean Gardner Named

Jean Gardner, wife of Governor Booth Gardner, has been appointed to Co-chair the Centennial Commission. Mrs. Gardner's interest in the Commission stems from her reading and study during the gubernatorial campaign. During the process of sorting out her goals as to what her interests might be when and if her husband were elected, Mrs. Gardner found the centennial plans and goals very exciting. "What a great idea for our state to have a major celebration all year long in 1989," Mrs. Gardner said. She

The importance of this Pacific connection was brought home to Mrs. Gardner at a recent meeting that she and her husband attended with a Trade Delegation from Sichuan, Washington's sister province in China, exploring the trade possibilities with the Orient so crucial to Washington's future.

Mrs. Gardner was involved with the Save Our Station efforts in Tacoma to find uses for the Union Station there. During campaign swings around the state, she found restored community

tion, most states have published books such as Idaho's *Directory of Idaho Foundations* and Washington's *Charitable Trust Directory*, which can also help you research foundations.

As in the case of foundations, northwestern states are not headquarters to as many corporations as eastern states, but many large corporations are centered here. Morrison-Knudson, Albertson's, Boeing, Boise Cascade, Weyerhaeuser, Crown Zellerbach, Simplot, Tektronix, Fred Meyer, and many other huge businesses call the Northwest home and donate thousands of dollars and many in-kind services annually to local groups. In some cases these large corporations even have their own foundations. Each state also has numerous small and mid-sized corporations that should be investigated. For example, the major banks in each state are usually generous corporate donors. Most corporations, like most foundations, have specific regulations concerning the types of activities they will fund. They tend to give money to projects that will in some way benefit them, through either services to employees or publicity in areas in which they do business. This is no more than fair and can be to your advantage if you convince a corporation that you are providing an opportunity to create good public relations for itself. Again, it is essential that you research corporations before seeking funds, and the state Foundation Center Library can normally assist you with this task. Some large corporations, like most foundations, have specific grant-application procedures. With most, however, it is best to make an appointment and plan to personally visit the corporate headquarters to discuss your plans and needs.

Each state has some sort of tourism commission, and these sometimes provide funds to communities and organizations which can demonstrate that their activities will increase tourism. Well-organized, properly advertised anniversary celebrations attract tourists, and your planning committee might be eligible for such funds. At the very least you should contact the tourism commission well in advance of your celebration to let it know of your plans because it may be able to help with free advertising.

Few state historical societies can afford to provide money to local communities and organizations. However, most have people on staff who can provide expertise in a wide variety of areas. Most often these services are free, although it may be necessary for the local committee to pay for travel expenses if a site visit is required. Further, the state historical society is a great referral office. It can put you in touch with other agencies that do provide funding for history-related projects, such as the state historic preservation office, which might be able to help you pay for a historical survey of your town or provide advice on renovating a historic building; or the state oral history office, which might help pay for oral history interviews. You should contact your state historical society very early in the planning process to see what types of assistance are available.

Each state has a variety of professional organizations that can greatly benefit communities celebrating anniversaries. In most cases state library or museum associations, universities, and departments of education cannot actually help finance a celebration. Frequently, though, they can provide valuable in-kind services — especially by making professional consultants available, often at little or no expense.

NATIONAL FUNDRAISING

There is an even wider range of funding sources on the national level, and you should consult the bibliography for assistance in learning more about these organizations and their interests.

Several federal agencies offer a variety of programs that can help pay for anniversary celebrations. Included in these are some well-known agencies and some that are not so well known. Among the former are the National Endowments for the Arts and the Humanities, which offer more programs and generally award larger grants than their state committees; the Institute of Museum Services, which provides financial support to American museums; and the National Historical Publications and Records Commission, which assists in the collection and preservation of historic documents. Several other often overlooked federal agencies can provide necessary financial assistance for your committee. For example, the Farmers Home Administration can provide loans for certain building projects; community development grants can be utilized to assist in historic preservation; and various Department of Labor programs can provide youth, senior-citizen, and unemployed workers for nonprofit organizations. The best historian's guide to federal agencies is Hedy A. Hartman, *Funding Sources and Technical Assistance for Museums and Historical Agencies: A Guide to Public Programs* — although, given the constantly changing nature of American government, it has become somewhat outdated since its publication in 1979.

There are numerous foundations and corporations that provide funds throughout the country. Again, it is best to consult your state Foundation Center Library for assistance in researching these sources. Many large national and international corporations will fund projects wherever they have plants or employees. Thus, while the Hewlett-Packard Company is headquartered in California, it might well fund a project in Boise, Idaho, because it has a company facility there.

There are numerous national professional organizations that can be of assistance in planning a local anniversary celebration. Included in this category are the American Association for State and Local History, the National Trust for Historic Preservation, the American Association of Museums, the American

Folklore Society, the Oral History Association, and the National Council on Public History, among many others. While most of these do not award grants, many publish helpful materials or can offer advice or professional assistance.

CONCLUSION

While some communities will support an anniversary celebration more readily than others, the ability to raise money is more often determined by such factors as enthusiasm and imagination. You need to determine realistically how much money is necessary to undertake the projects envisioned, then allow yourself enough time to raise the amount required. There is no guarantee your fundraising will be completely successful; but if you enter upon the project with sound ideas, realistic goals, and a positive attitude, you will have a good chance of succeeding.

NOTES

[1]Carl W. Shaver, "The Rights and Rituals of Fund Raising," *Museum News* (February 1973), 51:16.

[2]The quotation is from Dee Brown, *The Year of the Century: 1876* (New York: Charles Scribner's Sons, 1966), p. 10. Also see *Celebrating a 300th Anniversary* (Boston: Tercentenary Conference on City & Town Committees, 1931); and *The Report of the British Columbia Centennial Committee* (Victoria: The Committee, 1959).

[3]See *Report of the South Carolina Tricentennial Commission* (Columbia: The Commission, 1971), p. 159.

[4]David H. Stratton, interview with the author, Pullman, Washington, September 24, 1984.

3

Sample Project Activities

T he range of projects that can be undertaken to celebrate a centennial is limited only by the planners' imagination. This chapter is not a list of all possible anniversary activities. It includes a few general suggestions with detailed information on the planning involved for two project ideas, indicating the amount of time and effort required to successfully undertake such projects. The chapter is divided into two sections, one dealing with short-term activities and one with long-term projects. These terms refer to the lasting impact of the projects, not the amount of time required to plan for them. Thus a parade would be considered a short-term project because it is over with — and largely forgotten — in a day, while an anniversary supplement to the local newspaper is considered long-term because it can be read, and its impact felt, long after a single day of celebration. It is entirely possible, however, that a community parade will involve more planning time and the services of more people than a newspaper supplement.

A successful celebration should include both short-term and long-term projects. Too often anniversary celebrations lead to a single day or a few days of festivities, after which most people soon forget that the community even had an anniversary. An anniversary is an excellent time to educate people about their local heritage, and every anniversary committee should plan at least one project that will provide long-lasting benefits to the community.

SHORT-TERM ACTIVITIES

Short-term projects provide most of the "festive" aspects of the celebration and include such ever popular events as parades, reunions, beard-growing contests, concerts, races, dances, picnics, fireworks displays, rodeos, plays, and festivals. Keep in mind that some short-term events can utilize existing annual affairs, saving your committee time that can be used to organize other activities. For example, ask your local fair board to incorporate a historical anniversary theme into the annual county fair. If your area has an annual arts and crafts show, make this one of your anniversary festivals. If a local athletic group hosts a regular footrace, ask it to run the course near historical points of interest to give the anniversary-year race a special flair. Just as every celebration should include a project of lasting significance, so should each include a festive occasion such as those mentioned above. These activities will ensure participation by a large number of people and will help to publicize your other activities. The following are suggestions for less utilized short-term projects, divided into several broad categories.

Appreciating local architecture

The main streets and residential sections of even the smallest towns are filled with architectural detailing that too often goes unnoticed and unappreciated. Some say we have sacrificed building construction quality ("They don't build 'em like they used to") in our modern rush to erect houses and business buildings quickly and cheaply. If that point is debatable, certainly in many cases we sacrifice aesthetics for functionality. An anniversary celebration presents an excellent opportunity to reacquaint community residents with a time when buildings were constructed for both function and beauty, and a construction job was not completed until some fine architectural detailing was added to distinguish a building from its neighbors. A walk down Main Street or through an older residential neighborhood is like opening the door to an earlier time — it is, perhaps, our most accessible avenue to the past. Most people are surprised at the wealth of architectural detail found in their own home towns. Sure, Philadelphia has nice buildings, but what can Pocatello, Idaho, possibly offer? The reason for this feeling is that we are accustomed to viewing the world only at eye level. At eye level we might as well be in a shopping mall instead of on a small-town Main Street. False fronts have been added to "modernize" buildings; aluminum display windows have replaced their smaller wooden predecessors; glass doors have been added. Luckily for us, such renovations are expensive, and above this pastiche of modern contrivances usually sit one, two, or three stories of untouched architectural enjoyment. Take some time to cast your eyes above street level and let these "new" buildings speak to you, telling you about your town's history. Once you have gained this new appreciation, take the opportunity during the anniversary celebration to acquaint others with this well-kept secret. There are many ways to do so.

Architectural drawings have, in recent years, gained acceptance as true pieces of art. In almost any town some of these drawings still exist for a few of the original buildings. They may be at the historical society, in the town hall, or still locked in the vaults of the building they depict or its architect's office. Try to uncover some of these drawings, along with information about the architect, and form them into an exhibit, perhaps adding historical and contemporary photographs of the building. The exhibit can be in one central location,

Above: *Although the ground-level stories of most buildings have been remodeled, upper levels are usually untouched and provide windows to the past. This streetscape is in downtown Twin Falls.* (Idaho State Historical Society)
Below: *Tours of historic homes can serve a dual purpose, as educational programs and as fundraisers.* (Nez Perce County Historical Society)

such as a museum or community center, or divided among several storefront windows with each building housing a historical display of its own.

Once you have discovered some of the unique architectural details of your community, try to interest the rest of the town in seeking these out. Set up a photographic exhibit illustrating doorways or cornices and ask people to identify where these details are located. You can run a photograph of a different architectural detail each week in the newspaper under the caption "Where is this?" and provide the location in the following week's paper.

Another useful — if somewhat depressing — exhibit is to have a photographic display of buildings in your town that have been destroyed, together with photos of what replaced them. You will generally need little textual material to make a strong case for historic preservation.

Tours are also popular ways to tell the community about its architectural heritage — and raise money for the anniversary committee. The most popular are historic-homes tours, which can be planned for any community, although the owners' cooperation must be arranged well in advance. The Idaho State Historical Society Auxiliary in Boise and the Latah County Historical Society in Moscow have each sponsored several successful homes tours and found them not only good educational devices but excellent fundraisers as well. Equally effective, but done less often, would be a series of lunch-hour tours. Many people who work in our downtowns welcome the opportunity of a diversion during lunch time, and 20- or 30-minute architectural walking tours of the community can be planned, perhaps leading in a different direction each week for several weeks. Self-guided walking tours, for which people are aided by brochures, are another popular method of encouraging people to notice their architectural surroundings. Several Idaho communities, including Hailey, Lava Hot Springs, Mountain Home, and Sandpoint, have found this to be an effective way of generating community interest in local history.

Activities for youth

All anniversary celebrations should in some way seek to actively involve young people, for they are the ones who will have to preserve the community's heritage in the future. But they must first learn to appreciate it. Most youth activities would work well as school projects, although any youth group — Scouts, 4-H, church — can undertake projects centered on the anniversary celebration.

Children could compile lists of "My Favorite Things in Town" and then research the history of those "things" to determine why they are so special, and if they always were. They might research the life of one local individual — not necessarily someone well known — to find out what she would have worn, how he made a living, and what his or her house looked like at various stages in the community's history. Children might gather the history of their own families, interviewing relatives about family traditions, games, and superstitions. In fact, an anniversary celebration can provide the impetus to encourage people of all ages to get involved by preserving the stories of their own families. Children especially will be excited by knowing that history is not impersonal, that their own parents and grandparents were and are a part of the community's history.

Exhibits researched and designed completely by children not only teach them much about their town's past but serve as a popular way of involving many people in the celebration because everyone will want to come see what the children have created. During the Bicentennial, a fifth-grade class in Galveston, Texas, created its own "museum" that, though it was open for only a few weeks, was one of the city's most popular activities. A vacant building was made available to the students, and after a few days of clean-up they began deciding what would go into their museum. Some objects were made — drawings, papier-mache animals, and human figures. The children also brought objects from home and borrowed them from businesses, friends, the library, and the fire department. They wrote exhibit labels and printed announcements for the grand opening, when student guides led adults through the museum.[1]

During the New Jersey Tercentenary celebration a group of high-school students prepared a map of their town's history, marking all sites that were important at the time of incorporation. Another group prepared a map with the names of original town property owners, their acreages, and the dates of each land grant. These maps were duplicated and used as table placemats.[2]

Many youth projects lend themselves to use by school groups, and the key to any classroom project lies with the initiative and enthusiasm of teachers. Teachers are frequently overworked, and it will be easier for them to ignore your anniversary celebration than to participate actively in it. However, every school has enthusiastic teachers who are eager to offer new subject matter. These teachers should be identified early by the anniversary committee and their advice sought. The committee should inform school administrators of the celebration early in the planning stages. Ask the administration to run notices about the committee and the upcoming anniversary in school newsletters. See if you can speak about your plans at faculty meetings or teacher in-service days. Another way to identify interested teachers in small districts is to contact faculty members individually. In larger districts a form letter can be sent to teachers informing them of your plans and asking interested individuals to contact you. Usually school administrators will see that these are delivered to all teachers free of charge if you supply the school with enough copies for everyone.

Naturally, history and social studies teachers are the obvious ones you will want to involve. They may want to sponsor a local history contest, have a history fair, or bring crafts demonstrators or long-time area residents into their

The Nez Perce County Historical Society provides Lewiston-area students with hands-on experience learning about traditional skills and crafts of the area. (Nez Perce County Historical Society)

classrooms. But if the history teacher shows little interest in your plans, do not despair: any imaginative teacher can weave an anniversary celebration theme into his or her curriculum. For example, students in business classes can encourage local business people to collect and preserve their records, write histories or reminiscences of their businesses, and deposit these at the local historical society or library. Physical education classes might try out — or demonstrate to younger children — some of the traditional games of the area, like horseshoe pitching; run, sheep, run; tug-of-war; blind man's buff; leap frog; arm wrestling; tag; and hopscotch. Science classes can identify the types of animals, birds, and insects found in the area, or label downtown trees by their species. Music classes could perform an old-fashioned concert. Home economics students might stage an old-time fashion show or have a needlework competition with an anniversary theme. Library helpers could develop a bibliography of the literature and history of the area. English teachers might assign essays on local history topics. The quantity and quality of school projects is limited only by the imagination.[3]

Remembering the pioneers

Just as our celebrations should not ignore young people, neither should they exclude older members of the community. In fact, it is hard to imagine an anniversary celebration that does not in some way recognize the area's pioneers. While our celebrations should do more than pay homage to a romanticized pioneer past, nonetheless this is a time to recognize those older residents of the community who are too easily overlooked. Beyond this, it pays to involve older citizens in your plans because, as a group, they have much time and talent. Find out what organizations in your area are made up primarily of older residents. Senior-citizen clubs and organizations like the Odd Fellows, Veterans of Foreign Wars, and Daughters of the American Revolution are likely candidates. Take presentations to these groups, as well as to nursing homes and senior-citizens' centers, on a regular basis and seek their active participation in your various projects.

Of course, not all senior citizens in your area are pioneers of the region, and you may want to especially recognize long-time residents. Certificates or some other public recognition can call attention to all those residents of your community who have lived there for many years. Wallace, Idaho, made all residents 80 or older who had lived in the community 50 or more years "Honorary Centennial Chairpeople" and the local newspaper carried a story about each. Many of your community's pioneers may have moved away, and this can be an excellent time to invite former residents back to town for a few days of celebration. "Old Home Days" such as the successful reunion breakfast in Jerome, Idaho, during its diamond jubilee have been some of the more popular activities of anniversary celebrations. Special invitations can be printed and made available for people to mail to former residents with whom they have maintained contact. The records of schools, churches, and clubs provide good sources for the names and frequently the addresses of people who have left the community.

Exhibits

One of the most visible ways to celebrate a community anniversary is with one or more exhibits. This is an excellent way to involve all sectors and age groups because exhibits can be done by virtually anyone. This is not meant to be derogatory toward professional exhibit designers and museum curators. Certainly, the fine exhibits you see in many museums were not put together overnight by people with no experience. But good and informative exhibits run the gamut from a simple photo display to sophisticated dioramas with audiovisual effects. Somewhere in this range of possibilities nearly everyone can find a way to be involved in developing a community exhibit.

An exhibit is more than a display. The word "display" connotes store windows filled with rows of shoes or attractively outfitted manikins. Displays are meant to capture people's attention, usually in the hope they will buy something. A good exhibit incorporates the best features of a good display — attractiveness and eye appeal — while adding something else: interpretation. An exhibit must be more than a group of old kitchen utensils or cameras or tools neatly arranged in a display case. It must tell the viewer something about the objects being displayed. Usually this is done through interpretive labeling, and such labeling consists of more than what we too often find in local museums (such as "Old iron, donated by Jessie Smith"). Even the simplest exhibit should be educational and the viewer should depart with more knowledge than he brought to it.

The types of exhibits you can undertake are virtually limitless. As discussed earlier, grade-school children can develop them, as can senior citizens. Lawyers can do exhibits on the legal profession, displaying early law books and photographs. Every occupational group from farmers to doctors, bricklayers to crop dusters, can do the same. Exhibits provide one of the best opportunities to involve business people in your celebration because virtually every business has a store window or display case that can be utilized effectively. If every merchant in your town were to have a historical exhibit in his window for only a week, everyone would be truly amazed at the amount of interest suddenly generated in the business sector. People who had not been downtown for years, as well as visitors from neighboring areas, would come to look. And many of them would spend both time and money while there, which should be enough incentive to get business people to cooperate. Such was the case during the Wallace, Idaho, centennial, when virtually every business had a storefront exhibit. A slightly different technique was used in Caldwell, Idaho, but still served to attract people to town. Department stores loaned display cases for use during the 1983 centennial celebration. These were placed in the city hall as well as in all banks and savings and loans in Caldwell — a total of thirteen locations. Historic exhibits were set up in the locations each month, so that by the end of the year 130 displays had been on view. These exhibits attracted much attention and were one of the most successful aspects of the celebration.

A photographic exhibit of local house interiors over the years, or of family photograph albums, will attract widespread attention. You can exhibit past and present handicrafts from your community or show some of the towns' advertising memorabilia — thermometers, pens, buttons, silverware, calendars, rulers — and depict how these have changed. Exhibits of local art are popular, as are those which focus on items that were previously or are currently manufactured in your community. Exhibits about some of the eccentric or famous characters from your town are intriguing, but equally important are exhibits about ordinary life, such as men's and women's work clothing. Along these same lines you might have a photographic exhibit on some of the large houses in town, but consider also having one on "the small houses of our community."

Do not forget that history is ongoing. Thus, if you live in a rural area you might have an exhibit on early homesteading. Equally educational, however, would be exhibits on modern aerial crop dusting and mechanized harvesting. Exhibits can focus on fashions, recreation, education, even birth and death. Those depicting holidays, hobbies, and pastimes are always popular. In fact,

A traveling exhibit is one of the most effective ways to reach a broad audience.
(Idaho State Historical Society)

if you can think of a topic, you can probably think of a way to construct an
interpretive exhibit about it. Exhibits are one of the most effective, least expensive ways to add variety to your celebration and to involve a large number
of people.

Clubs, libraries, and churches

Libraries, churches, and clubs are vital cultural and social organizations in
communities of any size, and they should be encouraged to participate in the
anniversary celebration. Certainly any of them can develop exhibits detailing
their growth. Beyond that, club members might well want to participate in the
celebration with fundraising and public-relations activities. If the community
is to have a parade or festival, they can be there with a float to advertise their
club or with a booth to raise money.

Libraries can develop special programs and highlight books on such subjects as logging, agriculture, railroads, arts, crafts, local history, and architecture. They can sponsor an "Anniversary Reading Club" in which all members
are required to read at least one book about the state or local area. Anniversary celebrations are also excellent times to compile local history reading lists
and bibliographies to distribute to patrons. The public library might also use
the anniversary as an impetus to develop a local history collection. Both the
Boise Basin Library in Idaho City and the Ketchum, Idaho, Community Library
have demonstrated that local history collections can be gathered and maintained
by small-town libraries and that, once gathered, these materials will be used

frequently by patrons. Such collections not only provide a service to library users but greatly increase the community exposure a library receives.

Churches traditionally perform a dual role in communities as houses of worship and social centers. Too often a church's early role as a leading force in community development is overlooked. Churches should be encouraged to use the anniversary celebration as an occasion to tell their story in the community and to acquaint their congregations with their role in the history of the area. Church histories may be written; sacred music of the past can be presented in local hymn festivals; the anniversary logo can be used on church bulletins for the duration of the celebration; congregations can cooperate in a special tour of community churches; religious artifacts can be utilized in exhibits. When Filer, Idaho, celebrated its centennial it held a special all-church community service, the theme of which was "The Past Speaks to the Future."[4]

A miscellany of project ideas

Anniversary celebrations lend themselves to competitions — everything from beauty contests to beard-growing contests. There can be contests for artists and

The Wallace, Idaho, drilling and mucking contest attracted competitors from throughout the state during the town's centennial.
(Wallace Centennial '84 Committee)

photographers and ax throwers; for the best anniversary cake or the best anniversary exhibit or the best parade float. You can utilize the media for your competitions. For example, you might have a quiz contest on the local radio station or in the newspaper, asking questions about the area's history. Contests are useful even before the celebration begins, because you can utilize them to develop logos and slogans to be used throughout the celebration.

If your celebration is to last more than a few days, you can designate special days that emphasize the important role played by various groups. A Farmers' Day may feature plowing matches or demonstrations of old and new equipment. Industry Day provides an opportunity for open houses so that local residents can learn more about what is produced in the region. Merchants' Day could offer business people an opportunity for special sales, perhaps rolling back prices on some items 100 years. You might also consider having a special centennial community dinner at which foods commonly served in your area 100 years earlier become the menu items.

Anniversaries can provide the spur for a variety of different historical programs, from a lecture series to one-minute spots on television focusing on episodes of local history. The telephone company might issue a commemorative anniversary edition of the phone directory, the post office may apply approved commemorative cancellations on town mail, or you might host a special sporting event to draw people to town. Anniversaries are also a time to encourage people to undertake needed projects that really have nothing to do with history. Thus you might interest a group or club in beautifying a park as an anniversary project, or in painting downtown buildings. Take a look around your community and see what needs to be done, or what projects have been talked about for a long time with no concrete progress. An anniversary celebration is a time for a community to take pride in itself, and it is one of the best times to get people to do those little jobs that never seem to get done.

FAIRS AND FESTIVALS:
A CASE STUDY OF A SHORT-TERM PROJECT

Several Idaho communities have demonstrated that even in small towns community festivals can be successful and are an outstanding way of involving people in local history. The Owyhee County Historical Society's annual "Outpost Days" and the Latah County Historical Society's annual "Ice Cream Social and Old Time Crafts Fair" not only attract hundreds of participants but generate substantial revenue for the host institutions. A crafts festival is a perfect example of how a "short-term" project — one that is enjoyed by the public for only a day or two — can require long-term planning and preparation. It is usually best to begin planning for a crafts festival about a year in advance, especially if your group has no previous experience at organizing such an event. Even small affairs take much organizational and planning time, and a calendar of actions leading up to the event should be developed as soon as possible.

Crafts festivals generally demonstrate old or traditional crafts to the public. As such, they lend themselves naturally to an anniversary celebration program. They can be especially helpful in interpreting crafts and skills that have developed as a result of your area's natural surroundings — pine-needle basketry, obsidian artifact chipping, wheat weaving, and so forth. However, do not feel that you must limit yourself to only "old" crafts, because such a festival can provide an excellent opportunity to demonstrate how traditional skills are always evolving. Thus you might have both a whittler and a chain-saw artist at the same festival. The first thing the subcommittee in charge of the festival should do is decide upon the purpose of the festival. Is this to be a way of showing only traditional folk crafts to the public? Is the primary purpose to attract a large crowd and publicity? Is the festival to raise a significant amount of money for other anniversary projects? Of course, a festival can have a variety of purposes, but priorities should be set. If your primary purpose is to offer an authentic interpretation of how crafts were done in the "old days," you might not be able to have as large a festival or raise as much money as would be possible if you were not so stringent in your guidelines. By limiting your focus to old crafts done in the old way you will probably reduce the size of your fair, because many craftspeople in your area are probably expert at nontraditional crafts, or might use modern machines to undertake their task — such as a potter who utilizes an electric wheel.

Crafts festivals involve a large number of visitors, all arriving at once, and adequate planning is necessary to ensure that such crowds can be handled. It is a good idea to have the volunteers who will work during the day walk through the site to get a feel for traffic flow, determine the places where crafts demonstrators can set up, and so forth. Other aspects require careful planning, too.

Inviting demonstrators

Most craftspeople, especially professionals, are extremely busy. They make most of their money during the summer months — when you will probably want to host your fair — because most such festivals are held outdoors. It is necessary to contact potential exhibitors well in advance so they can reserve the date of your event. The more demonstrators you want, the earlier you will have to invite them, because there are always many who will not be able to participate. Do not feel your work has ended once the craftspeople say yes. You must contact them periodically, preferably in writing, to remind them of the festival, learn how much space they require, and determine if they have any special needs — such as water, electricity, and shade. It is also a good idea to have a few "back-up" demonstrators, if possible, in case there are last-minute cancellations.

Fundraising

Many festivals are not intended to make money, and for obvious reasons these are the most easily organized. If you want your festival to be a fundraiser, you have more questions to answer. Will you charge an admission fee for visitors, or rely on donations? If you charge an admission you need a site with controlled access, such as a gate or door. If you rely upon donations you will need to have a conspicuous site for your donation container, and you should have a large, visible sign — perhaps stating a suggested donation level. It is also helpful to assign a person to staff the donation area. This person can greet and thank people and answer questions. Will you charge a fee for exhibitors' booths, ask for a percentage of sales, or allow exhibitors to keep all profits, if any? If you charge a booth fee you will eliminate many potential exhibitors because nonprofessionals might not want to pay. If you encourage craftspeople to sell their work you might end up with little demonstrating because the exhibitors will naturally be busy trying to market their products. Another way to make money during a crafts festival is to host auxiliary events at the same time, such as the selling of refreshments or the hosting of a raffle, if state and local laws permit. The Internal Revenue Service has not definitely ruled upon what is and is not taxable income from crafts fairs, even when they are hosted by non-profit groups. You should contact your regional IRS office for a ruling during the planning stages. You will also need to determine whether state taxes are applicable and get a tax certificate if necessary.

Crowds

If your event has been well publicized you should expect to attract a large crowd. After all, this is why you have spent all that time planning. But crowds present management problems. Exhibitors' booths must be located in such a fashion as to facilitate traffic flow. At the same time, you must avoid a location scheme that tends to isolate some exhibitors from the traffic flow. Restroom facilities should be available. Many communities have local ordinances requiring a given number of restrooms for certain sizes of crowds, which may necessitate renting portable restrooms. If admission is to be charged, you will need to have an adequate number of ticket sellers and the proper amount of change for the crowd expected. You might need to have directional signs or a central information booth. It is essential that you discuss your festival plans

Authentic traditional crafts demonstrations are helpful in interpreting historical subjects. (Folk Arts Program, Idaho Commission on the Arts)

with your city staff and police and fire departments. Permits may be required to host such an event and you will want to be prepared in case an emergency arises. You may be required to have on-site medical facilities, and you should make sure you have adequate liability insurance. No doubt some members of your crowd will need handicapped access of various types. You should also make provision for adequate nearby parking or utilize a shuttle bus to get visitors to the site.

Weather

Most festivals are held outdoors and their success is dependent as much upon the weather as upon adequate planning and publicity. You can increase your odds of good weather by knowing local weather patterns. If June is traditionally a rainy month, July mild and dry, and August overly hot, schedule your event in July. Be sure, though, to make certain your festival does not conflict with other, longer-established activities. If the day of the festival arrives and it is rainy you have several options:
— You can cancel the affair, but this can lead to extremely bad public relations.
— You can have a rain date announced in advance. This can cause problems, though, because many exhibitors are busy all weekends, having reserved only one for you. Further, enthusiasm is diminished and you can never expect as good publicity — or as large a crowd — on a later date. Nor is there any guarantee it will not be raining then, too.

— You can move the festival indoors. This is a viable option only if your community has the indoor facilities to handle the size of crowd and number of exhibitors you were planning for outdoors.

— You can host the event as planned anyway, rain or shine, at the location planned on. This is generally the best policy. If necessary, tents and awnings can be rented or borrowed to protect some of the exhibitors and crowds. Be sure to reserve these in advance. In fact, it is often a good idea to reserve them anyway, as they are helpful on hot days as well as rainy ones.

Concluding the festival

The event is not over until a previously designated clean-up crew makes the grounds as clean as they were before the festival began; all exhibitors and volunteers have been thanked in writing; and all festival committee chairpersons have written and filed reports about what went right and what went wrong.[5]

LONG-TERM ACTIVITIES

Anniversary celebrations have traditionally provided the impetus for the completion of projects with significant long-term benefits. When Portland, Oregon, celebrated the centennial of the Lewis and Clark Expedition in 1905, it constructed the largest log structure in the world as a tribute to Northwest forestry. British Columbia built its Provincial Museum, one of the finest in the West, as part of its centennial celebration. The Lewiston, Idaho, centennial of 1961 gave that city the Luna House Museum, now the Nez Perce County Historical Society. As part of the American Revolution Bicentennial celebration a history of each of the fifty states was written and published, representing the first major historical work on some states that had been done in generations.

Your anniversary committee will work many hours preparing for its celebration. It would be a shame if all of that effort went into projects with no more lasting significance than a Fourth of July fireworks display. The committee owes it to itself to have at least one long-lasting memento of the celebration. In many instances, it is also easier to recruit volunteers and donations for long-term projects than for short-term ones. "Really interested citizens will often give willingly of their time and their money," wrote Walter Dunn in *Local Historical Celebrations*, "but they will want to see lasting fruits of their efforts."[6] And the community will be better served if it is able to learn more about the region than is possible if only short-term projects are undertaken.

As with short-term projects, there is no lack of possible ideas for lasting anniversary activities that can be undertaken in virtually any community. These

Above: *The Idaho State Historical Society's annual "Museum Comes to Life" celebration features a variety of craftspeople and demonstrators and draws large crowds to the Society's museum.* Below: *The Owyhee County Historical Society's annual Outpost Days includes demonstrations of skills such as wheelwrighting.* (Both, The Idaho Statesman)

can range from very grandiose undertakings to small but significant projects. Some of the best, and often least expensive, long-term projects are those that use the enthusiasm generated by an anniversary celebration to gather and preserve materials and information relating to an area's history. Appeal to people to search their storehouses, attics, and trunks for letters, diaries, manuscripts, newspapers, and other local history materials. During its sesquicentennial in 1966 Indiana had a very successful "Hoosier Treasure Hunt" to undertake just such a search for valuable historical documents. Much of the collecting was actually done by grade-school students throughout the state who encouraged friends and relatives to donate or loan written or printed records pertaining to Indiana history. All materials were forwarded to the state library. If items had not been donated, they were photocopied and the originals returned to the owners. The governor authorized cash prizes to the counties generating the most documents. Thousands of valuable materials were thus gathered in a short period and have been preserved for future research. Such gathering projects can also be done on a local level. Utilizing a small grant from the Association for the Humanities in Idaho, the Boise Basin Library in Idaho City in the early 1980s undertook a successful project to gather and catalog diaries, reminiscences, and other valuable published and unpublished materials relating to the history of the Basin. Similar projects have been used to gather photographs and museum artifacts. A project entitled "South Carolina in Your Attic," not tied to an anniversary celebration, was sponsored by the Department of History at the University of South Carolina in 1984. The project focused on a series of workshops aimed at helping people identify valuable historical objects and encouraging them to preserve the artifacts or donate them to museums or other agencies equipped to preserve such material. The key to any successful gathering project is to convince people that their mother's letters, father's work clothes, or family snapshots are truly valuable historical materials that ought to be preserved.[7]

Some gathering projects can be more labor-intensive than those mentioned above and require a larger volunteer force. Tombstones contain a wealth of historical data — genealogical information, the popularity of certain names at different times, evidence of disasters and catastrophes — that is often lost because of weathering of stones, vandalism, and improper maintenance. The transcription of this information is a valuable historical project. In Idaho, the Latah County Genealogical Society transcribed every readable tombstone from every public and private cemetery in the county, indexed the records, and made them accessible to researchers. This project has greatly assisted Idaho genealogists and historians. An anniversary committee could also encourage people to write their family histories or reminiscences and deposit these in the local historical society or library. The planning committee might want to encourage an oral history project in which members of the community are interviewed about their lives in general, or about specific topics of local significance. Once recorded on tape, these interviews can be indexed, perhaps transcribed, and made available for research. Several small organizations in Idaho — including the Bonner, Latah, and Upper Snake River Valley historical societies, the Clearwater Historical Museum, and the Caldwell Public Library — have undertaken large, professional-quality oral history projects on very limited budgets.[8]

Many communities want to find ways to "get local history out to the public," and there are many effective ways to do so. Several towns have undertaken the task of marking significant historic sites as part of an anniversary celebration.

Gravestones such as this one, in a Wood River Valley cemetery, contain a wealth of information that can be transcribed and preserved as a valuable anniversary project. (Folk Arts Program, Idaho Commission on the Arts)

There are a number of firms in the West that specialize in constructing vandal-resistant outdoor historical markers and signs, but local groups can often complete such a task with volunteer labor and the donation of needed materials from a building-supply house. One county in New Jersey adapted a school bus into a traveling "Historymobile" for the year of the state tercentenary celebration in 1964. For a number of years the Idaho State Museum of Natural History has had a Museum on Wheels set up in the trailer of a donated tractor/trailer rig. Such historymobiles provide an effective means to reach broad audiences, but fuel and driver expenses can be high even if vehicles are donated or loaned.

A less expensive but effective way of reaching a wide audience is to develop a slide show. This can be a traditional slide program with a narrator or it can be a program in which a narrated tape is synchronized with the slide show, making it possible to send the program out to groups unaccompanied by a narrator. It is also possible to type a narrative, marking places where slides are to be advanced, so that a club member, teacher, or other person can simply read the text and advance the slides appropriately. Slide programs can range from these simple endeavors to sophisticated multi-projector programs. Keep in mind also that in many schools and libraries videotape is replacing the slide projector as a way of presenting programs. Audiovisual experts at colleges or public schools can help you select the proper equipment and advise on how to develop an effective audiovisual presentation. Many individuals now have video cameras and may be willing to volunteer time to videotape a program; but be sure they have the expertise to do a good job.

Anniversary celebrations are an excellent time to encourage local schools to undertake projects of long-lasting significance. For example, students might decorate buildings in town with murals depicting area history. This not only serves to teach local history to students but also can be a way of beautifying downtown as part of the celebration. Pullman, Washington, grade-school students have placed dozens of murals portraying historic events and people on exterior walls of local businesses, and the project has been so successful the students have not been able to fill all the requests for such artwork. Local history essay contests in which prizes — perhaps donated by local businesses or civic organizations — are awarded to winning entries are also valuable school contributions. Completed essays should be deposited in the local historical society or library for permanent research use. Most western states now participate in National History Day Fair, and such essays done for the anniversary celebration could also be entered in that competition, if they fit into the annual History Day theme. In fact, it is a good idea to check with your state History Day coordinator, because he or she often has a wealth of project ideas suitable for school children.

Perhaps the most valuable contribution to schools would be to use an anniversary celebration as inspiration to include more local history in school cur-

Elementary-school children in Pullman, Washington, have decorated many downtown buildings with murals depicting scenes from the community's history. The project has involved the schools and the community at large in a joint preservation and beautification project. (Keith Petersen)

riculums. This is an excellent time for teachers to work with representatives of historical societies and knowledgeable area residents to develop teachers' kits and expand or alter curriculums, so that students will have as much opportunity to learn about the development of their home town as they have to learn about a place like Philadelphia. The Mountain Home, Idaho, centennial celebration of 1984 was a joint effort of the Mountain Home schools and local residents, producing several slide/tape and videotape programs on the local area that are now permanently available for use in classrooms. In addition, the planners conducted several workshops on how teachers could incorporate local history into their various curriculums. During the Bicentennial the Latah County Historical Society and the White Pine School District in northern Idaho jointly shared expenses in publishing five booklets to be used in grade schools. Each booklet recounted the life story of an early resident of the county, as recorded during the historical society's oral history project. The booklets have since been used by all schools in the county.

Anniversaries often provide an occasion for historic preservation or restoration projects. Buildings that have been neglected for years can become the focal point of a community celebration and can be preserved for the use and enjoyment of future generations. One of the best ways to develop enthusiasm for a restoration project is to undertake a program to educate the public about the area's architecture. Significant structures in the community can be carefully photodocumented and the resulting photographs can then be deposited in a historical society or library. The best photographs, perhaps combined with existing architectural drawings of the buildings and a brochure detailing their histories, can then become the nucleus for an exhibit on the community's built environment. Preston, Idaho, for example, commissioned a local artist to do pen-and-ink sketches of local structures during its centennial and then utilized these in a handsome and educational exhibit and publication. Guidebooks or brochures for walking or driving tours can also be provided to inform people of their architectural heritage. Such photodocumenting, exhibiting, and touring in themselves are valuable anniversary tasks, but the architectural project can continue as enthusiasm for preservation increases. Businesses may be encouraged to paint and fix downtown buildings. Or one building in town may be chosen for a community-wide restoration project. During the time that such preservation enthusiasm is generated, local residents can be encouraged to contact their State Historic Preservation Office for advice and help in adding local structures to state historic inventories or the National Register of Historic Places. The completion of such nominations provides a permanent record of a building, and registration often encourages the preservation and restoration of structures.

One of the more popular permanent outgrowths of anniversary celebrations — often spurred by a desire to preserve a significant building — is the organization of a community museum or historical society. In many instances, museums and historical societies begun as part of an anniversary celebration have thrived and become important parts of a community. Unfortunately, too many communities decide to begin a museum or historical society in the excitement of an anniversary celebration without giving thought to the long-term financial and personnel commitments such organizations require. There is a misconception on the part of many people that museums and historical societies are synonymous terms. A museum collects, preserves, and exhibits three-dimensional objects. A historical society may or may not have a museum as one of its public services, but it can do much more than merely operate a museum. It might maintain a research library, collect oral histories, and publish books, for example. Museums and historical societies have one thing in common — to be successful, they must have long-term commitments of financial and volunteer assistance. The easiest part of operating a museum or historical society often is obtaining a building in which to house the operation, since nearly everyone can get enthusiastic about supporting a building drive. It is much more difficult, however, to keep the utilities paid, hire staff, and develop programs on a permanent basis.

Anniversary celebrations can provide the impetus for many diverse projects that will have long-lasting benefits. Some — such as recording information from tombstones — can be completed during the celebration itself and the results of the work made permanently accessible. Others — such as establishing a museum — can only be started during an anniversary celebration and require a permanent community commitment in order to be successful. All require careful planning and much time, and none should be undertaken without propper consideration of whether your community will be able to provide the commitment necessary to complete a project successfully. The bibliography at the end of this handbook will provide assistance to those considering some of the long-term projects discussed here.

PUBLICATIONS: A CASE STUDY OF A LONG-TERM PROJECT

Even in the age of video, the best way to produce a lasting memory of your anniversary celebration is to publish some type of written document about your area. While some observers are justly concerned about the declining interest in reading, local history publications seem to be gaining in popularity. If adequately planned, a local publication can not only serve as a handsome, permanent tribute to the anniversary celebration, it can be a fundraiser as well.

Traditionally, groups planning an anniversary publication think automatically of a community history, but other types of publications can be equally valuable and popular. Consider a cookbook, for example, or a book focusing on historic photographs of your area. The republication of out-of-print local histories, maps, or novels with a local setting can all be very popular. While a published local history bibliography will have less sales potential than the other publications cited above, it can have a tremendous local significance. In 1983, for example, the Kootenai County, Idaho, History Project published a *Historical Reference Guide to Kootenai County, Idaho*. This annotated bibliography was not sold, but reference copies were distributed to libraries throughout northern Idaho and eastern Washington and it has become a valuable resource for scholars, teachers, genealogists, and others interested in north Idaho history. Several historical organizations in Idaho have published walking-tour brochures or pamphlets designed to enhance exhibits and have found these to be popular and effective ways to increase awareness of local history. During the Oregon Centennial of 1959, the state history committee published seven strip maps, one for each of the major highways crossing the state, marking and giving brief descriptions of historic sites along the way. Such maps can be produced for a local vicinity or a county. Your group might also think about writing material for a newspaper supplement or a series of historical feature articles rather than publishing a work of its own.

Many items must be considered by groups planning a local history publication. Some of the most important are discussed below.

Establishing a goal

If your goal is to make available to the public an invaluable piece of historical literature, you may want to publish an entirely different type of manuscript than if your primary goal is to make money. Of course, you can meet both expectations with one publication. Too often people think "good" history connotes stuffiness and boredom. The best history is both very readable and well researched. However, it is entirely possible that you will decide the most valuable lasting contribution you can make is to publish a bibliography, research guide, local diary, or some other type of material that does not have a large sales potential. This is a worthy goal, but, given today's ever increasing printing costs, such a book may not recoup expenses. You must take such realities into account when planning your publication.

Obtaining a manuscript

Whether republishing an out-of-print book or publishing a new one, careful recruitment is necessary. Talk to librarians and bookstore operators about the kinds of material that are in demand. If you are planning to reprint, you will need to determine if the out-of-print publication will help you meet your goals. Just because something is old and "interesting" does not mean it is worthy of expensive republication. Be sure to check copyrights before republishing anything.

If you are recruiting someone to write a new book for you, be sure you are confident they have the research and writing skills necessary to produce the quality of work you want. Nothing is more embarrassing than recruiting a manuscript only to reject it when completed because it is inappropriate or inadequately researched or written. If you are not familiar with the author's work, ask to see writing samples.

You may be able to find a volunteer to undertake your writing task. A local person with an interest in your area and a willingness to help your cause might write your book. A university student who can receive college credit for his or her work, or turn the research into a thesis, is another possibility. Remember, though, that local historians have to pay bills and must make a living just like everyone else. We rarely think of asking a doctor or plumber to volunteer his or her professional services, but too often we think historians are in the field only as an avocation, not a vocation. If at all possible you should try to pay any writer — even the local "volunteer" or university student — an honorarium or fee, and you may have to enter into a contract to pay an author for his or her services, just as you would pay any other professional. Because few local

The Latah County Historical Society received permission from a major publisher to reissue a novel about the county that had been out of print for forty years. Dressed up in a new dust jacket, it sold 2,000 copies. (Idaho State Historical Society)

history publications reach mass markets, it is unlikely you will be able to entice a writer only by offering royalties or a percentage of the profits.

Editing

Every good author needs a good editor, and you should make it clear to your author that his or her work will be edited. Of course, substantial editing should be done only in consultation with the author, for it is his or her name that will appear on the cover. It is usually best to have an editorial committee or group of readers thoroughly go over the manuscript. Possible members of such committees include English teachers, newspaper editors, librarians, and local historians. Though an editorial committee is an excellent idea, there should be only one ultimate authority on style and language. Thus, there can be several "readers," but only one "editor."

To ease the editing job, have the manuscript come to you doublespaced with wide margins to allow for editorial comments. Having all drafts typed on word-processing equipment will save time and money in the long run, as the work may go through three or more drafts. Once the author has provided you with a manuscript, you should make enough copies so that all members of your editorial committee can review it simultaneously to save time. Some readers will make only grammatical or stylistic changes, but at least one reader with a background in historical methodology and local history should review the text for accuracy.

Once all editorial comments are received, the manuscript copies should be returned to the author who can incorporate them into a rewrite. Remember that writing and editing is a give-and-take affair that requires good dosages of humor and compromise. The author will not agree with all the suggested changes and the editorial committee needs to be flexible, for there is no "right" way to write a book. Most changes will be minor and can be readily agreed upon. The author may have to meet with the editorial committee to reach a compromise on more substantive suggestions.

If your committee chooses to republish an out-of-print work, remember that it is not ethical to edit these. However, you may choose to add a new introduction or other new sections, or add explanatory footnotes to make the work more understandable to modern readers.

Quality of finished product

Eventually you will have a manuscript that is ready to be printed. While the quality of your finished product will largely be determined by your budget or by the amount of donated services and materials you receive, you should always strive to have the best finished product you can afford. There is a law of diminishing returns in book publishing, and very high-quality books are usually slow sellers because they are expensive. On the other hand, aiming for a certain level of quality will actually help you sell books: even if they have to pay a few dollars more, most people would rather buy a book that is typeset and permanently bound than one that is mimeographed and stapled together.

At the lowest end of the budget, you can have your final manuscript typed on a good electric typewriter using a carbon ribbon. This "camera-ready copy" can then be run on an offset printing press and the final product, which can include photographs, will look quite good. Once the manuscript is printed you will have a number of binding options, which can be explained by your printer. You can even lay out and design your own book to save money. Be sure, however, to get lessons from someone experienced in the use of basic design tools such as light tables and straight edges so that your finished product looks as professional as possible.

If you have more money, you will want to investigate the possibility of hiring a professional designer and having the book typeset. These expenses, as well as such factors as paper quality, number of copies, number of photographs, and the type of binding, will dictate the price of the finished product. Printing is not cheap, but remember that you are making a valuable addition to your community's history as well as producing a keepsake.

Solicit bids from as many reputable designers and printers as possible. To do this, seek professional advice on how to write your job specifications. Once these have been typed, run off as many copies as you need and send the *same* specifications to each firm. Your final choice of a designer or printer should not be dictated by cost alone; the lowest bid is not necessarily the best. Investigate the bidding firms and ask to see examples of former work. Quality should always be a determining factor in your selection.

Once you have selected a firm, enter into a written contract. Both parties must know what is expected before work commences.

Paying the bills

It cannot be overemphasized that publishing is an expensive undertaking. In most cases you will have to pay all of your bills before you begin marketing the book. This can cause some cash-flow problems, but it is unfair to ask your author, designer, or printer to wait for payment while you try to peddle your books. You will need to have cash on hand before you begin your publishing project.

There are several ways of financing a publication. If a book is only one of several activities planned for the celebration, other fundraising projects can be undertaken and the proceeds placed in a publication fund. Local businesses, clubs, individuals, or foundations might be willing to underwrite part or all of the publication costs. These donors are then usually acknowledged within the publication, unless they desire anonymity. You will often find it easier to solicit such contributions if the potential donor views your publication as important to him. Thus, if your book is to deal heavily with local forestry history, a lumber company might be willing to underwrite some or all of the costs. You can also offer pre-publication sales to build up a publication fund. Usually people are offered an incentive for purchasing their copies in advance, such as a reduced price or a special limited hardbound edition. Businesses or individuals may subsidize the publication if allowed to purchase pages and write their business or family histories as part of the book. Unfortunately, this usually leads to a less-than-uniform final product and is often more distracting than beneficial. It also suggests, perhaps inaccurately, that businesses or individuals have had editorial control over the text of the book itself. Depending upon the publication, you may want simply to sell display ads. If you are certain you will be able to sell enough copies to pay back the loan, you may find financial institutions willing to make a low- or no-interest loan for such a project.

As part of its multi-faceted centennial celebration, Hailey, Idaho, produced a seventy-page booklet on the town, written by historian Florence Blanchard and published by a local newspaper. (Idaho State Historical Society)

Marketing

Even if you do not intend to make a profit you need to invest a certain amount of energy in marketing, for there is no sense publishing a book that is not read. Too often groups congratulate themselves upon a fine job once a book is published and do not consider marketing a necessity — apparently thinking the book will "sell itself," which never happens.

A separate marketing subcommittee should be formed and should begin work at least a year in advance of the publication date. This subcommittee should seek inventive ways to whet people's appetites for the book even before it is published. When your group contracts with an author, send a news release to local media outlets. Have your author be on the lookout for interesting vignettes about local history that could be written as newspaper stories. The author or someone from the marketing subcommittee can make appearances on radio or television. You can develop a slide show or traveling exhibit to tell people and groups about the upcoming book.

Naturally, marketing will intensify once the book is published. Find as many outlets as possible to sell the book for you. Bookstores are an obvious choice, but do not ignore supermarkets, hardware stores, and the like. Send out review copies to all local newspapers and magazines. Also send review copies to state and regional history magazines and journals. Try to have the book read by local book-discussion clubs. Offer to have the author discuss the project as a program for area civic organizations and clubs. Produce posters advertising the book. It may be worthwhile to pay for advertising in carefully selected newspapers, magazines, or radio stations, perhaps jointly with local bookstores. Brochures mailed to prospective buyers can be an effective marketing tool. It is important, though, that you carefully develop your mailing list, for a shotgun mass-mailing campaign rarely pays. Members of the local historical society, high-school graduates who have moved away, and friends of the author are good groups from which to begin drawing your mailing list. You can usually sell a good number of copies to local and regional public libraries, as well as to university, public school, and historical society libraries. It is customary to provide a discount to such institutions.

Perhaps the biggest mistake made by first-time book publishers is to underprice their books. As a rule of thumb, you need to at least double your unit cost in order to make a profit. In other words, if you publish 2,000 copies of a book and your expenses — author's fees, design and printing costs, advertising, and so on — make each book, or unit, cost $10, you should sell your book for at least $20. This seems extravagant at first glance, but really is not. In fact, it is a bare minimum, and large publishing houses add a much heftier amount to the price of their final product. Remember that you will be giving away several free copies — at least ten to the author, several to reviewers, and perhaps some to special friends, donors, or public institutions. Remember also that most bookstores or other outlets will want to make some money for handling your book, and discounts to them generally run from 10 to 40 percent. You may choose to hire a book distributor to help with marketing, and these firms generally expect to make at least 50 percent on each copy sold. You need to investigate your market before settling on a final price. See how much your local bookstore wants before it will handle your product. Find out how much it will cost to mail copies to those who order from out of town. Determine how many free copies you want to distribute. You may even find it necessary to more than double your unit price. Of course, if your expenses have been underwritten and you do not want to make a profit, you can set your price accordingly.

Printers will tell you that your unit cost will decline as you print more copies. This is true, for the bulk of the expense is in getting the manuscript camera ready and having the initial run printed. After that, you are paying only for paper and printing-press time. Thus, the unit price of 500 copies of a book might be $10, but the unit price of the next 500 might be only $2, meaning the unit price for the 1,000 copies you will receive will be only $6. However, if you realistically believe you can sell only 500 copies it will be unprofitable to order an additional 500 merely to bring the unit cost down. No one makes money when books remain on storage shelves, unsold. You should plan on selling the bulk of your books during the first year after publication. Do not order an extra allotment for "tourists" or "newcomers." That is an unprofitable, unrealistic marketing plan and you will eventually find that the only way you can get rid of your books is to offer substantial discounts or give them away. Remember, too, that it is better to underestimate than to overestimate your audience, for you can always do a second printing. If you retain your camera-ready manuscript and make no changes in it, or if the printer is willing to store the plates, the unit cost of books in the second printing will be substantially lower than in the first printing.

Many people see publishing as a sure-fire way to make a profit. Actually, as printing costs have risen in recent years, publishing as a profitable venture has become quite risky. This does not mean you cannot make money at it, or that you should shy away from publishing, for books are still valuable treasures worthy of the efforts of any anniversary celebration committee. However, you should test your market in advance as much as possible. No doubt others in your area — or nearby areas — have published local history materials. Find out how many copies of what kind of book, and at what price, they have sold. Do some informal polling. Ask friends and acquaintances if they would buy the book you intend to publish, at the price you have projected. Try to come up with a realistic figure of how many copies to print. If your community has a population of 10,000 do not expect to sell 5,000 copies of a town history. Not every family will want a copy, and you will find a very limited market outside the city limits.

There is no finer way to pay lasting tribute to an anniversary than by publishing a book on local history. When you enter upon your task in a businesslike, professional manner, you will help ensure the quality of your final product.[9]

NOTES

[1]*Galveston* (Austin: Texas Commission on the Arts and Humanities; Washington, D.C.: American Revolution Bicentennial Administration, 1973), pp. 11-13.

[2]Robert C. Hartje, *Bicentennial USA: Pathways to Celebration* (Nashville: American Association for State and Local History, 1973), p. 103.

[3]Those who wish to involve schools in their festivities should consult *Your Classroom and the Bicentennial* (Helena: Montana Bicentennial Administra-

tion, [1975?]), which has hundreds of innovative ideas for classroom projects focusing on an anniversary theme.

[4]Madeline Buckendorf, "Centennials and Diamond Jubilees: Some Project Examples," *Working Together Newsletter* (Idaho State Historical Society) (Fall 1982), p. 1.

[5]Two excellent publications are highly recommended for people planning crafts festivals. See Daniel Reibel, *Craft Festivals: A Planning Guide,* Technical Leaflet No. 117 (Nashville: American Association for State and Local History, 1979), and Joe Wilson and Lee Udall, *Folk Festivals: A Handbook for Organization and Management* (Knoxville: University of Tennessee Press, 1982).

[6]Dunn, *Local Historical Celebrations,* Information Sheet No. 20 (Manlius, New York: Regional Conference of Historical Agencies, [1975?]).

[7]See Linda Gates Vandivier, *A Time to Celebrate* (Indianapolis: Indiana Sesquicentennial Commission, 1966), p. 23, and *South Carolina in Your Attic: Exploring the State's Hidden Historical Resources* (Columbia: Department of History, University of South Carolina, 1984).

[8]Both Idaho and Washington have published directories of oral history projects in their states. These are very helpful to people planning an oral history project because they provide valuable contacts. See Madeline Buckendorf and Elizabeth Jacox, *Directory of Oral History Resources in Idaho* (Boise: Idaho State Historical Society, 1982), and Margot H. Knight, *Directory of Oral History in Washington State* (Pullman: Washington State University Oral History Office, 1981).

[9]The best guide for groups wishing to undertake a publication project is Thomas E. Felt, *Researching, Writing and Publishing Local History* (Nashville: American Association for State and Local History, 1976).

4

Publicity

A successful anniversary celebration requires the dedicated effort of many people working on many committees, and all must function effectively. It is difficult, however, to imagine a more important group of people than those undertaking publicity, for you do not want to throw a party to which no one comes.

Too often publicity is deemed an insignificant part of celebration planning. Activities are arranged and committee members naturally assume people will attend. Overworked committees put off publicity until the last minute, thinking a late blitz will lure crowds. Unfortunately, most media outlets are too busy to provide publicity for unexpected events, and many people are unable to attend activities they did not schedule in advance. The publicity committee should start meeting when anniversary planning begins, and the committee should ideally be made up of people who have no other responsibilities for the celebration so that they can devote full time to publicizing events.

Some groups choose to hire a professional publicity firm, as did Wallace, Idaho, when celebrating its centennial in 1984. The professionals hired by Wallace did an outstanding job, generating substantial regional and even national publicity. If you decide to hire professional consultants, make a careful study of firms available and ask the same types of questions outlined in Chapter 2 for hiring professional fundraisers. Most small towns will not have resident publicity firms, but the state tourism committee, the chamber of commerce in a larger community, or other such agencies should be able to refer you to professional publicists. It is not necessary that the publicity firm be located in your immediate vicinity but it should be relatively close by or willing to have a representative in your community on a regular basis, because the local anniversary planners will need to meet often with the publicist. Hiring professionals does not guarantee a better job than you could do yourself, and it by no means ensures preferential treatment by the media. It is wise to have a written agreement with the publicist on areas of responsibility and expenses. The most common types of arrangements for hiring professionals — whether publicists, fundraisers, or others — are:

—retainer: the professional is paid an annual, monthly, or seasonal fee to cover year-round activities;

—hourly or daily rate: the professional agrees to be "on call" when needed and will charge according to time expended, possibly with a prearranged limit;

—fixed fee: a lump sum is agreed upon for a specific assignment.

If outside publicists are retained, they must begin their work early, just as a volunteer publicity committee would.

Should you — as most groups will — decide not to hire a publicity firm, select the members of your publicity committee carefully. Try to involve media professionals, such as newspaper reporters or people who work in radio or television. These people are often too busy to serve on a permanent publicity committee but are more than willing to lend advice. You may decide to form a special advisory committee made up of such people, which will meet only occasionally to lend guidance to the permanent publicity committee. Other valuable additions to such an advisory committee include graphic designers, members of area nonprofit groups with experience at undertaking successful publicity campaigns, and representatives of local businesses.

Publicity and fundraising are in many ways similar. In fact, good publicity can help make for good fundraising. Many of the basic generalizations about fundraising outlined in Chapter 2 also apply to publicity. For example, the publicity committee should have a knowledge of the area and the types of projects that have previously received good attention in the media. Committee members should speak with others who have undertaken successful publicity campaigns. They should research their press outlets and determine the habits and idiosyncracies of the various media in the area, then supply press releases accordingly. Perhaps most important, they should have active imaginations, for the variety of publicity possibilities is just as broad as the variety of fundraising activities.

One of the first things the committee should do is develop a slogan and design a symbol or logo for the anniversary. These symbols and slogans should then be used in all publicity about the celebration. The more they are used, the more people will associate the anniversary with a certain slogan or logo, and the more times people see these emblems, the more they will be reminded of the upcoming activities. A slogan should be catchy, suitable, and short. For its Tercentenary, New Jersey used the slogan "For Three Centuries: People, Purpose, Progress." Illinois' Sesquicentennial slogan was "Celebrating 150 Years of the Good Life." The slogan for Wallace, Idaho, was very concise and descriptive: "Celebrating 100 Years of Wallace Mining History."

The committee should develop a distinctive logo or symbol that can be used on posters, buttons, billboards, brochures, and stationery and in various other ways. The committee may want to recruit the assistance of professional designers

One way to develop an anniversary logo is to hire a professional designer, as Wallace, Idaho, did. Both Caldwell and Rexburg, Idaho, had community-wide contests to design the best logo; Rexburg's winning design was then polished by a professional artist. (Idaho State Historical Society)

to produce this logo, but perhaps an even more effective method of developing a slogan or symbol is to have a community-wide contest with money or other prizes awarded to the best entries. Not only will this generate a diversity of ideas from which to choose, it will also serve as a way of creating interest — and publicity — within the community, getting people to think about the upcoming celebration.

Once a logo and slogan have been developed, the publicity committee may choose to protect them by trademark or in some other way control their use so that vendors must receive permission to utilize them. The question of whether to control the anniversary symbol must be carefully considered. Most anniversary committees do attempt to control symbols. This can also serve as a means of fundraising, since vendors are often required to purchase the rights for use or pay a percentage of sales. Some committees, however, believe this defeats the purpose of having a symbol. The Wallace Centennial Committee, for example, not only allowed free use of its symbol but openly encouraged such use. The result was a much wider dissemination of the symbol on a broader range of products than would have been possible otherwise, and a consequent increase in publicity.

The publicity committee should, at the earliest possible date, develop a publicity schedule. Timing is essential to good publicity. If news is released too soon, people will forget; if too late, they will not have time to plan. The publicity time schedule should list all the publicity you plan, in order of occurrence. It should also specifically detail every publicity assignment and should include the names of people responsible, clear statements of assignments, and deadlines for completion of tasks.

The primary emphasis of the publicity committee will be to secure press coverage of the celebration. Newspapers and radio and television stations are businesses operated for profit. These media outlets receive many more requests for space and time than they can economically grant. They have no obligation to carry your story unless it is newsworthy, and you will be competing with many other groups who feel they are just as deserving of space and time as you. While there is no way to ensure that your story will be covered, there are some things you can do to improve your chances of coverage.

The publicity committee should make a list of media contacts to whom press releases will be sent. Each newspaper, television station, radio station, and magazine in your vicinity — or in your target area if you want to attract crowds from a greater distance — should be contacted and the names and titles of people who are to receive news releases determined. Always send releases to a specific person, as that is more effective than if they are just sent to the "News Room" or "Public Service Director." A short personal cover letter sent with your news releases often helps establish rapport. One person on the publicity committee should be designated as the press contact person. Members of the press are sometimes understandably confused if a number of different people from the same organization contact them regarding news stories.

Keep your news releases as concise as possible. Do not go into exhaustive detail. Use the five "W's" as a guide: who, what, why, when, where — and sometimes how. Do not attempt to be cute when writing a news release — just state the facts and be sure they are accurate. You will draw more attention to your celebration if you have a series of small news releases rather than relying on one big story. Appendices C and D at the back of this handbook provide a sample news release and public-service announcement.

Whenever possible, attempt to include photographs with news releases to newspapers and magazines. Good-quality photographs are always sought by the print media, and these draw attention to a story much more than does a mere column of words. Submit only black-and-white glossy prints, no smaller than five by seven inches. Attach an identification to the photograph, taking care not to deface the image with fingerprints or by writing on the back. When mailing, protect the print with cardboard. Be prepared to relinquish the photographs you submit, as they cannot always be returned.

Depending on how many media outlets you will need to contact, you may find it helpful to develop press kits. Such kits can include photographs, a brief history of the community, a statement concerning the goals of the anniversary committee, lists of the various committee members, and a schedule of events. If you hope to receive more than local media coverage, contact your state's bureaus of the Associated Press and United Press International wire services, which are located in state capitals and larger cities. You can send information of statewide interest to be carried in newspapers throughout the state.

Be sure to provide complimentary tickets to your events to members of the press. Not only does this serve as a way of thanking them for their help, but, if you are having a celebration that lasts over a period of time, this technique will also help with publicity: most members of the press will want to write about what they saw. In addition, be sure to let radio or television stations know of comments you receive about any publicity or news carried over the air, for station managers are vitally interested in audience response.

There is always considerable discussion over whether to utilize paid or unpaid publicity devices. The beliefs that "you get what you pay for" and that the press is "obligated" to cover your celebration are both simplistic and naive. Media markets vary widely. A celebration that would be front-page news in McCall, Idaho, might only warrant a small paid advertisement in a Portland newspaper. The press has no obligation to cover your event unless it is newsworthy. Fortunately, in most communities a major anniversary is a special event, and you should not find it difficult to garner press coverage if you begin working with the media early. If you are planning a whole series of events spread over a year, it is unreasonable to expect the press to cover each event to the extent necessary to ensure large attendance. This is where the judicious use of paid advertising can be helpful. Also, keep in mind that even if the press does not cover your story as a news item, there are generally ways of getting free publicity. Most newspapers have community calendars and many have entertainment pages that are especially suited to your type of event. Further, although the Federal Communications Commission no longer requires it, most radio and television stations still provide free public-service announcements for nonprofit organizations. These range from short notices that are simply read on the air to sophisticated "spots" that are produced for you by the station or professional media consultants. Check well in advance with media outlets to determine what types of public-service announcements they may be able to provide and use.

The Latah County
Historical Society's
10th Annual

ICE CREAM SOCIAL

AND

OLD TIME CRAFTS FAIR

July 28, 1985
1-4 p.m.

-Live Music
-Museum Exhibits
-Benefit Raffle
-Crafts Demonstrations
-Horse and Wagon Rides
-Vintage Automobiles
-Contest for Best Period Costumes
-Sale of Local History Books
-Flower Displays

"An Old-Fashioned Way
To Spend a Summer Day"

Non-professionally designed handbills and flyers, done with a typewriter that has variable typefaces and with embellishments available at most print-shops, can be produced inexpensively and help to advertise coming events. (Idaho State Historical Society)

The type of press campaign your committee utilizes will be largely determined by your media market, your budget, and the sizes and types of activities you plan. You should not be afraid to pay for some advertisements if you believe the return will be worth the investment. And do not waste your time complaining if the press does not cover your events as well as you believe they should. If you work with the local media and discover their needs and wants, you should have a good indication of what they will be able to do for you and can plan accordingly. Most publicity committees will, in the end, want to have both paid and free media notices. The proper mix can be determined only by understanding the local media market.

You should plan on advertising your anniversary celebration in places other than the press, using a diversity of publicity to reach the widest possible audience. Posters are a traditional and successful method of advertising, and a well-designed, eye-catching, strategically placed poster will be noticed. People must be able to read them quickly, so keep the design uncluttered and the information to the point. Posters need to be in areas of heavy pedestrian traffic to be worthwhile. Posters that compete with too many others, are poorly lit, or are placed at the wrong level for easy visibility are not worth the time and effort of posting. Among the places you can usefully place posters — after seeking permission — are shopping centers, department stores, banks, civic centers, schools, and libraries.

Brochures, flyers, and handbills are also helpful. These can be placed in motels, restaurants, libraries, and bank lobbies and near store checkout stands, and they can be mailed out as invitations. It is sometimes possible to have flyers enclosed with mailings of other groups, such as those sent out by clubs, retail stores, banks, and utility companies. As with posters, avoid trying to say too much; hold copy to the essentials. Make the brochures look just as good as you can afford to.

Many groups find it helpful to have posters and brochures designed by professionals. The investment is usually worth the expense in terms of a high-quality product; but again, investigate firms and ask for examples of previous work before entering into a contract. Remember that all such work takes a considerable amount of time, so provide materials to designers several months before the finished products are needed. Among the essential items to include on posters are the names, dates, and locations of events. In addition to this basic information, brochures may contain a more detailed calendar of events and acknowledgements of people and businesses who have assisted. A professional design is not always essential. If you can afford a professional, fine. However, if you believe a poster or brochure is critical, but cannot afford to hire a designer, do not go without. Utilizing press-on letters available at most office-supply stores, a typewriter with a good carbon ribbon and a variety of typefaces, some good-quality line drawings or photographs, and a little patience, nonprofessionals can produce very effective products.

Once posters or brochures are designed and a logo or symbol developed, the publicity committee should investigate other ways of utilizing this investment in artwork. You may want to produce stickers, decals, buttons, tokens, street banners, or bumper stickers — all of which can be made and distributed months in advance of the celebration as some of the earliest forms of publicity. Your goal is to get the word of the celebration to as many people as possible, so be imaginative.

The anniversary publicity committee might want, as one of its first actions, to develop a speakers' bureau, identifying people who can talk to organizations and clubs about the upcoming celebration. Most organizations are eager for good programs, and mailing a letter to all area groups concerning your speakers' bureau will generally result in a good number of engagements. These talks can be augmented with slides or even slide/tape programs. Be sure your speakers are good before sending them out. Warn them not to talk too long

— twenty to thirty minutes is usually a maximum. And remember that clubs usually schedule speakers well in advance.

Another very effective way of getting the word to a large number of people is to develop small traveling exhibits describing the celebration, which can be placed in high-traffic areas such as malls or stores. These exhibits, along with the speakers' bureau, can serve as an effective method of early advertising.

It is a good idea to produce an occasional newsletter concerning celebration plans and activities. It should be mailed to all members of the various committees as well as to volunteers to keep everyone up to date on the planning process. Newsletters can also be mailed to members of the press, libraries, schools, clubs, and governmental officials and in this way can double as publicity devices. Do not let a small budget make your newsletter so unattractive that it goes unread. Avoid the tendency to fill every space with words; condense articles and leave some white space. While mimeographing remains the least expensive way to produce a newsletter, offset printing costs are generally low enough to be affordable by most groups and modern photocopy machines produce excellent copies. Any committee with a good typewriter can produce professional-looking newsletters at very little cost utilizing an offset press or photocopier. This method also allows for the use of photographs, for even snapshots can look amazingly professional.

In addition to newsletters and brochures, the various anniversary committees will be sending and receiving a good amount of mail, so a special post office box is in order. You can even use your post office box as a form of publicity if you are able to pick a key box number. For example, a community celebrating its centennial in 1986 might want to have post office box number 1886 or 1986 or 100.

There are many existing advertising devices that the publicity committee can utilize at no expense. For example, state and regional tourism committees often publish calendars of events and will be happy to include your activities. These are usually printed well in advance, so it is best to check with these agencies as soon as your dates are set. Other forms of regional advertising include magazine event calendars, airline magazines, and the regional "community calendars" frequently sent with bank notices and utility bills. On a local level, the chamber of commerce frequently produces a community calendar, and most schools, clubs, and organizations, as well as many businesses, have "in-house" newsletters that will run notice of your activities.

The publicity committee should work as much with area business people as it does with the media, for businesses can greatly assist in advertising anniversary activities. They can post notices of events on bulletin boards, have special displays in store windows, announce events on outdoor signboards, and decorate their buildings with bunting or banners. If you work carefully with

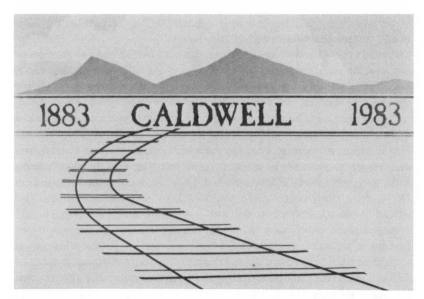

Above: *Caldwell's centennial poster was the winning entry in a community-wide contest for students.* Below: *One very visible part of Jerome's Diamond Jubilee was the gathering and reproduction of old photographs from the community.* (Both, Idaho State Historical Society)

business people, you will find that frequently they will be happy to mention anniversary activities in their media advertisements, providing the committee with some free "paid" advertising. Often businesses are pleased to go to considerable expense to help publicize an anniversary if they are given enough advance warning and if they believe it is to their advantage in terms of increased revenue or community good will to do so. For example, special anniversary shopping bags or milk cartons might be printed. Restaurants may pay for anniversary menus and placemats that include event schedules; hotels and motels may do special mailings to patrons, providing discounts or special packages to out-of-town people attending the celebration. Do not be afraid to ask businesses for help. They will be among the primary beneficiaries of a successful anniversary celebration and have a vested interest in seeing that large crowds are lured to town.

The best form of publicity in most small communities is still done by word of mouth. People will begin talking about the upcoming celebration and making plans to attend if the publicity committee lays a firm advertising foundation upon which enthusiasm and expectations can be built. Be enthusiastic — it is catching. At the same time be honest, for exaggerations and half-truths can cause extremely bad public reaction. Be accurate and meet all deadlines.

Once activities are completed, the publicity committee should send written thank-yous to everyone who helped publicize the event. Brief notes will help maintain the good will generated by your celebration and will make it easier for those community organizations that plan activities after you to receive good publicity.

Good publicity does not just happen — it is the result of hard work and many hours of time. If your celebration is adequately publicized, it will be virtually impossible for any resident of your community not to be aware of your activities.

PUBLICITY CHECKLIST

☐ Begin planning early
☐ Appoint separate publicity committee
   ☐ Carefully select committee members
   ☐ Decide whether to use a professional publicity firm or volunteers
☐ Develop slogan and/or logo
☐ Make early contact with local media
   ☐ List all media contacts
   ☐ Press kits
   ☐ News releases
   ☐ Complimentary event tickets to members of the press
☐ Be imaginative in investigating other types of publicity
   ☐ Paid advertising
   ☐ Posters
   ☐ Brochures, flyers, handbills
   ☐ Bumper stickers, decals, buttons
   ☐ Speakers' bureau
   ☐ Traveling exhibit
☐ Investigate free local, regional, and state publicity outlets
   ☐ Tourism committees
   ☐ Chambers of Commerce
   ☐ Airlines
   ☐ Schools
   ☐ Clubs and organizations
   ☐Businesses
☐ Publish a newsletter to keep all committees and the community informed
   of anniversary plans and activities
☐ Thank all who helped with publicity

5

Documenting the Celebration, Concluding the Celebration, and Building on What You Have Begun

Many excellent anniversary celebrations take place for which adequate funds are raised, outstanding projects undertaken, and large crowds gathered. Too often, however, the organizers of these celebrations forget one key element in their planning: they do not make a systematic effort to document their activities. At the conclusion of the celebration they find themselves wishing they had photographs, clippings, and other materials attesting to their good work. Sometimes a frantic search is undertaken, asking friends and members of the community to donate memorabilia as part of a permanent record. Such a system of haphazard collecting is never as satisfactory as collecting systematically throughout the planning and implementing stages of the project.

It is important to document your activities for a number of reasons. First, your anniversary celebration will become part of the community's history, and a historical record should be maintained. Second, other people in the community — or in neighboring areas — will someday want to have a community-wide celebration, either as an annual event or to mark another significant anniversary. You will greatly aid their efforts if you maintain a comprehensive record of your celebration so others can determine what went right and wrong. Third, it will be an enjoyable exercise for your anniversary committee members, upon completion of the celebration, to sit back and browse through the accumulated clippings, photographs, and souvenirs, congratulating themselves on a job well done.

One of the first tasks of the central planning committee should be to appoint a person who will be in charge of gathering all documents and artifacts relating to the celebration. Depending upon the size of the celebration planned, this person — often called the "historian" — may want to form a committee to assist him or her.

The historian should begin gathering materials as soon as planning begins, for you will want to document how you arrived at decisions to undertake certain projects as well as how the projects themselves turned out. Generally there will be newspaper stories covering early planning activities that should be clipped. Be sure to note the source and date on these clippings. If minutes of committee and subcommittee meetings are taken, arrangements should be made to give these to the historian once the committee has disbanded. Further, copies of all correspondence concerning the celebration written by committee and subcommittee members should be maintained. Once this correspondence is no longer useful as part of a working file, it should be given to the historian.

The historian should also make arrangements to document the celebration visually. Photographs should be taken not only of the activities themselves but also of people working on the celebration, in committee meetings, dress rehearsals, autograph parties, and so forth. It will normally not be necessary to hire a professional photographer for such work, but the volunteer enlisted should be competent. The historian may decide to have some of the photographs taken in color, or even as color slides if they can be used to publicize the celebra-

Some local libraries collect and properly maintain manuscript and oral history materials dealing with their communities. They are suitable depositories for the records of anniversary celebrations. The Ketchum, Idaho, Community Library has an active oral history program, with space for storage, cataloging, and transcribing materials. (Ketchum Community Library)

tion. The majority of photographs should be black and white, however, as this film has a longer life span than color. Black and white is also cheaper to reproduce in any subsequent publications. It might also be useful, especially if there are too many events for one photographer to cover, to ask other people to donate copies of their photographs. The historian should have a complete file of photographs — and negatives — once the celebration is over.

There are parts of almost all celebrations that lend themselves to tape recording. Significant speeches, musical performances, and the like should be recorded and preserved. If a speech has been written out, the historian should also attempt to obtain a copy of the text. Not only is it important to preserve such materials for documentation, but they can also become valuable educational tools. For example, texts or recordings of significant lectures or of an original local history play can be deposited in libraries, used in school curriculums, or published in the newspaper. One aim of such documentation is to allow certain events to be repeated, reaching an even larger audience. In addition, the historian may want to tape a few interviews with key committee members — or even members of the general public — to get their reaction to the celebration. Such candid interviews often provide the best background on what went right and wrong and are therefore excellent planning tools for the future. It will probably be most convenient to make such recordings on a portable cassette machine. Keep in mind, though, that such tapes should eventually be transferred to more permanent reel-to-reel tape for longer keeping and that most cassette tape machines are technically unable to record music as adequately as are more expensive reel-to-reel recorders.

There are many other materials that should be gathered by the historian. Multiple copies — probably between three and five — of all publications produced as part of the celebration should be preserved. These include not only such items as books and pamphlets, but also posters, handbills, advertising brochures, and play programs. Copies of all souvenirs and commemoratives should also be saved. Scripts or recordings of radio programs, videotapes of television shows, and newspaper supplements should likewise be gathered. If the celebration is to be publicized on a statewide or regional basis, the historian may want to hire a clipping service to collect all newspaper releases. These clipping services can be located by checking the Yellow Pages in larger cities.

Once the celebration is over, the historian should have a large collection of artifacts, correspondence, photographs, clippings, and other materials thoroughly documenting the festivities. The committee must then decide where to deposit these items for permanent safekeeping. In fact, the central planning committee or historian should begin negotiations with potential depositories even before the celebration is concluded so that the final location of the records has already been determined. An early consultation with potential depository sites can also be beneficial to the historian, because people working at such facilities are generally aware of the types of records worth preserving and can help the historian plan his or her collecting program.

The final disposition of the anniversary records will vary from community to community. The anniversary planning committee should ask two key questions when determining where to deposit materials: (1) where will the materials be best preserved for the use of future generations? and (2) which facility can best provide access to the materials so that they can be studied and used by others? A third important consideration is to attempt to retain the records as close to home as possible so that they are conveniently located for the use of community residents.

You would not buy a car without a test drive, nor should you select a depository site without first seeing it. It is perfectly legitimate to make a thorough inspection of a depository before deciding to donate records. Are there volunteers or staff members who have expertise in properly preserving research collections and in assisting the public in using them? Are research collections maintained in special areas so that they will not be excessively handled — or stolen — by the public? Are materials stored away from sunlight and in a room that does not have extreme fluctuations in temperature, both of which cause deterioration? If at all possible, the site selected should store its research collections, both paper products and artifacts, in special acid-free containers — file folders, envelopes, and/or boxes — as this prolongs the life of materials. Such acid-free storage items must be specially ordered but are not overly expensive. The anniversary committee might well want to purchase these items itself — or make a donation to the depository — to ensure adequate preservation.

The first thing that should be apparent upon selecting a depository is that the worst site for depositing records is in somebody's house or the filing cabinet of a local business. Tons of valuable historical documents are lost each year because they are stored in such a careless way. Businesses change hands and new owners see no value in retaining the "junk" of an anniversary celebration. Individuals die or move and their files are thrown away. If materials are not thrown out, they often deteriorate to an unusable state because few businesses or individuals can afford the time or materials necessary to preserve a collection of such documents and artifacts permanently.

There are several possible depository sites that should be investigated by the historian or planning committee, and most will have strengths and weaknesses. In many communities, the most likely spot to deposit the materials is at the local historical society. Many historical societies have both museums and research libraries and are therefore equipped to preserve a wide variety of formats, from three-dimensional souvenirs to paper to tape recordings.

If your community has a historical society that adheres to generally accepted professional standards of preservation and dissemination of research collections, it is the most logical place in which to deposit your materials. A historical society need not have a paid staff to be "professional." Many top-notch organizations are run by volunteers. Similarly, a paid staff is no guarantee that a historical society is run professionally. Unfortunately, many small historical societies are really that in name only. They function more as social clubs than as serious organizations dedicated to the preservation of valuable documents and artifacts. Further, many local historical societies are really only museums and do not know how to care properly for archival research materials.

If the local historical society is not suitable, another possible depository is the community library. This is a stable location and, as most people searching for information begin their research at the town library, materials deposited there would be used. Many small public libraries, though, are not equipped to handle specialized collections, such as a group of anniversary celebration papers and artifacts. Small public libraries generally deal almost completely in books and maintain their collections on open stacks, accessible to browsing and handling by their patrons. Such a system is adequate when a library deals only with books, which can be replaced, but it is an inadequate system for storing one-of-a-kind archival materials. Few public libraries have people with archival training on their staffs. Further, most libraries have no provisions for the maintenance of artifacts, such as souvenirs.

In many instances a university or college library is a suitable place to deposit materials. These libraries sometimes have librarians with archival experience on their staffs and may have specialized storage areas for archival materials. Frequently, though, college libraries — particularly at small colleges — are no better prepared to handle specialized collections than are public libraries, and they suffer the same shortcomings.

The anniversary committee should keep in mind that the first two considerations outlined above — adequate preservation of materials and ready access — are more important than the third — maintaining the collection close to home. If there is no appropriate depository within the community, the closest suitable site should be considered. In most cases this will be a state historical society or a large college or university.

Some committees, upon concluding their celebrations, find they have a deficit or surplus of funds. If the committee has planned adequately, there will not be a large budget deficit. If you are running into financial difficulties during your celebration, it is better to scale down your activities or bolster your fund-raising immediately than it is to conclude the celebration with a large deficit. It is always difficult to raise money once an event is over. The enthusiasm is gone, and potential donors have little incentive to help bail you out since they will receive little, if any, publicity for their contributions. A cardinal rule of anniversary planning is to reach the celebration's conclusion with a budget surplus, balanced books, or, at worst, a small deficit. If you do have a small deficit you can normally find people or organizations who will help you balance the books even after the events have ended. It is imperative that all bills be paid, however. Nothing causes worse public relations or hampers future similar activities more than to "end" a celebration without paying the bills in a timely fashion. Committee members may have to dip into their own pockets or plan additional fundraising events to relieve deficits. This is only fair, because in most instances if the committee had planned adequately there would be no deficits.

On a more positive note, many central planning committees upon the conclusion of festivities discover to their pleasure that they have budget surpluses. At times this is a planned occurrence, as many anniversary committees begin their celebrations with the raising of funds for long-term projects as a goal and may even have determined in advance the recipients of these funds. At other times, a central committee finds it has an unexpected budget surplus. The committee should not disband until it has developed a plan for disposing of this revenue. The spending of this money should receive the same thought and planning as did any of the celebration events, for such money was generated within the community and should be utilized for the good of the community. Some celebrations are so successful that events first held as part of an anniversary become annual activities. In this case, the committee may choose to use its surplus for the planning and implementation of the next year's events. Some committees donate the funds to a historical society, school, or other nonprofit group or offer it to the community in the form of scholarships. If the sum is substantial, the committee may want to hold a public meeting or poll organizations and individuals to get ideas about how the community wants to spend what is actually its money.

In addition to making arrangements for the final disposition of records and eliminating budget deficits or spending excess revenues, the anniversary planning committee has another vital task before it disbands. It must thank all those who assisted in making the celebration a success. In addition to written letters of thanks, the committee can print certificates of appreciation, send news releases to the local press, or have a special awards banquet.

A successful anniversary celebration will awaken a considerable amount of community pride and interest in local history. This is a time to build upon what you have begun. Your committee may decide to begin a museum or historical society as part of its anniversary celebration. This and other long-term projects will require long-term care and work, and the anniversary committee should see that such provisions are made before disbanding. An anniversary can provide the impetus to successful yearly activities that will keep community interest aroused and garner tourist revenue. The anniversary planning committee members, as well as the documents preserved from the celebration, are outstanding resources for the planning of such activities.

There is a tendency among anniversary planning committees to disband and relax too soon. Once a successful celebration has been completed, many committees naturally assume their work is over. Certainly the committee needs to congratulate itself and disband at some point, but there are always tasks that need to be completed even after the crowds have gone home. The committee should plan in advance for these chores so that tasks like writing thank-you letters, paying bills, and ensuring the preservation of documents are not forgotten. Further, organizations and individuals can struggle for years and not raise as much community interest in local history as is generated during an anniversary celebration. Do not let this community consciousness die as suddenly as it began. The anniversary planning committee will perform a great community service if, before disbanding, it works with other groups and organizations to develop ways of ensuring that interest in the community's heritage continues.

DOCUMENTING AND CONCLUDING THE CELEBRATION: A CHECKLIST

☐ Select a historian
☐ Begin gathering materials when planning begins
☐ Items to collect and preserve include

☐ Minutes   ☐ Handbills
☐ Clippings   ☐ Play programs
☐ Correspondence   ☐ Souvenirs
☐ Publications   ☐ Videotapes
☐ Brochures   ☐ Lecture texts
☐ Posters

☐ Arrange to have events photographed
☐ Tape-record suitable events
☐ Conduct oral history interviews after events
☐ Decide where to deposit archival materials
☐ Possible depositories include

☐ Local historical society
☐ Community library
☐ University or college library
☐ State historical society

☐ If there is a budget deficit, determine how to pay all bills in a timely fashion
☐ If there is a budget surplus, determine how to spend excess revenues
☐ Thank everyone who assisted
☐ Plan ways to build enthusiasm for long-term community good

6

Some Sample Celebrations:
Rexburg, Wallace, Jerome

T he three case studies which follow demonstrate that while there are some universal rules for undertaking an anniversary celebration, there is also much opportunity for catering to individual community needs. The towns examined range in population from 3,500 to 11,500, and each undertook a highly successful, very visible anniversary celebration.

In many ways these case studies are more notable for their similarities than for their differences. In each case, planning began well in advance of the anniversary. Each planning committee worked diligently to generate publicity. Each celebration was diverse enough to appeal to a large segment of the area's population, and each relied heavily upon a great number of volunteers. Each celebration lasted for a considerable period of time, rather than just a day or two. In each town, the central planning committee encouraged participation by area clubs and organizations, instead of attempting to plan all activities itself. In fact, the Jerome central committee planned no activities and instead served solely as a coordinating and publicity body. In no case did the central planning committee attempt to undertake too many projects itself — believing that concentrating on a few well-organized activities was better than trying to do too much.

There were other similarities as well. Each celebration demonstrated that historical anniversaries generate a considerable amount of tourist trade and revenue, and each was enthusiastically supported by business people. Schools, churches, and civic and social clubs played vital roles in each community. Each town developed a logo and theme, often through community contests. No town hired an outside fundraising or planning group to assist in its celebration, although Wallace hired a professional publicity firm — a firm from a neighboring town and well familiar with Wallace. Each community, in other words, relied on home-town people who knew their area to plan and successfully complete their celebrations. With the exception of Jerome — where various individuals kept scrapbooks — each central committee provided for documenting its celebration.

While there were many similarities among the celebrations, there were some differences. In Rexburg the primary group pushing the early celebration planning was the local historical society and in Jerome the historical society and its individual members played vital roles in planning. In Wallace the primary motivation came from the business community, although most of these business leaders had a strong interest in local history.

Because of the different makeup of the various committees, different long-term benefits derived from each town's anniversary. The strong influence of the historical society showed in Rexburg when that town published a history book, put money into restoring the city's Tabernacle — which is now the headquarters for the historical society — and aided the society's oral history and photograph collections. In Jerome, local historians gathered historic photographs for the historical society and revived interest in a town museum. In Wallace the long-term benefits were slightly less tangible: primarily an increased community pride and an awareness on the part of merchants that local history is good business.

Only Rexburg had a goal of making money from the anniversary, with profits designated for the Tabernacle restoration and oral history and photograph projects. Wallace raised only the amount of money needed to successfully undertake the celebration, and the Jerome central planning committee raised no money at all, relying upon the chamber of commerce for small contributions when needed, and asking each organization to plan and pay for its own activity.

The case studies that follow, then, demonstrate that certain basic rules should be adhered to in order to complete a successful celebration. But they also show that there is much room for individual adaptation. Most of all, they demonstrate that a successful anniversary celebration is the result of hours of hard work on the part of many dedicated, enthusiastic individuals.

THE REXBURG CENTENNIAL, 1983*

Rexburg is a town of about 11,500 residents in eastern Idaho. It is the seat of Madison County and, as the largest town north of Idaho Falls, serves as a trade center for a wide area. The town's primary economic base has always been agriculture, and predominant crops are potatoes, grain, and hay. Rexburg is the home of Ricks College, founded in 1888, which has an enrollment of 6,500. Operated by the Church of Jesus Christ of Latter-day Saints (Mormon), it is the largest private junior college in the United States. Other major economic

* Information for this sketch comes primarily from an interview with Louis Clements, chairman of the Rexburg Centennial Committee, conducted by Keith Petersen in July 1984. Additional information comes from two issues of the Upper Snake River Valley Historical Society's quarterly journal, *Snake River Echoes,* devoted to the centennial. See Volume 12, numbers 1 and 4 (1983).

concerns include Diet Center, Inc., founded here in 1970, which still maintains
its international headquarters in the town and employs over 400 full-time people. Art Porter, Inc., makers of "Stationery for the World," is also headquartered
near Rexburg and has a work force of over 750 people. An American Potato
processing plant employs about 350 people.

In March of 1883 a group of Mormon pioneers, under the leadership of
Thomas E. Ricks, moved into the region and surveyed the town of Rexburg.
Their charge from the church headquarters in Salt Lake City was to "go into
the Snake River Country, found settlements, care for the Indians, . . . gain influence among all men, and strengthen the cords of the stakes of Zion." By
the end of 1883 over 800 people lived in and around Rexburg and their numbers
grew to nearly 4,000 by 1890. Although there have been other denominations
in Rexburg, the town has always had a large majority of Mormons.

The impetus for Rexburg's centennial celebration began with a committee
from the Upper Snake River Valley Historical Society, which is headquartered
in the Rexburg LDS Tabernacle, built in 1912 and no longer used by the church.
The historical society's committee, concerned that the city was doing no planning of a celebration for the upcoming centennial, began meeting in early 1982
and in the course of that year planned most of the events that made up the highly
successful celebration. In December, 1982, Rexburg's mayor appointed a centennial committee headed by Louis Clements, director of the historical society.
The mayor also officially proclaimed 1983 as Rexburg's centennial year. In the
opinion of Clements, this committee should ideally have been selected two years
earlier; had it not been for the preliminary planning done "unofficially" by
the historical society, the celebration would not have been as large or successful.

The official centennial committee was made up of representatives of service
clubs and the business community, and a representative from the college, the
public schools, the city, the historical society, and the community (non-Mormon)
church. One of the first decisions faced by the committee was whether to hire
an outside consultant to plan the celebration. The mayor asked a Philadelphia
consultant to speak to the group, but when the committee heard his fee would
be $14,000 they decided to undertake the celebration themselves. Throughout
the project, work was done with an abundance of volunteer assistance and a
minimal budget.

The centennial committee never incorporated as a nonprofit organization and
actually received and spent very little money directly. A grant was awarded
by the Idaho Travel Council to produce buttons and brochures, but this money
was channeled through the city government. Similarly, many expenses were
covered either by donations of materials or by businesses paying bills directly.
Though the centennial committee did open a checking account, it only wrote
a few checks.

Funds raised during Rexburg's centennial went to the restoration of the Rexburg Tabernacle, which houses a regional historical society. (Upper Snake River Valley Historical Society)

"The key to the success of our centennial," Clements noted, "was involving people." Approximately 1,000 volunteers actively participated in planning and carrying out the various activities. This volunteer assistance was necessary because the committee had no budget, and no local tax money was spent on the celebration. The historical society provided seed money, which was later repaid by the centennial committee. In addition, donations came early and helped substantially. The Soroptimist Club made a quilt that was auctioned for $1,500. The Diet Center print shop published souvenir programs for a community play at no cost to the committee. These were sold, with proceeds going to the committee. A black-powder club arranged for food donations for a buffalo barbeque that made over $2,000. The celebration eventually cost about $50,000, but all expenses were raised by ticket sales and donations, and the centennial activities actually turned a profit of nearly $20,000. These funds were donated for the restoration of the Rexburg Tabernacle as well as for the historical society's oral history and historical photograph collections. Clements maintains that with adequate planning any community can host a large and successful anniversary celebration with only a small beginning budget.

The centennial committee decided to have a year-long celebration to make town residents more conscious of their history and to aid in promoting Rexburg as a place to visit in 1983. One of the first activities of the committee was to sponsor a contest to design a centennial logo. A $25 cash prize was

given to the winner, whose entry was then polished by a professional designer
and used on all brochures, souvenirs, and posters to advertise the celebration.
The chamber of commerce, some local businesses, and individuals also used
the logo on stationery. The committee willingly allowed anyone to use the logo
but reserved the right to 10 percent of the profits on sales of souvenirs utilizing it.

The committee decided early that it wanted to sponsor a few big events rather
than a large number of small ones. Thus it eliminated such ideas as having
bake sales or producing a centennial coin as ways to raise money. It chose not
to diffuse its energy, believing a few large events would successfully raise all
the revenue the committee needed. Five events were chosen: the writing of
a centennial history; a centennial ball; a community musical; a buffalo barbeque; and a centennial history program. These events were very successful, and
it was the belief of the committee that more major activities could have been
a strain on the volunteers.

The committee picked a chairperson for each major event. These chairpersons then appointed their own subcommittees and functioned largely in-
dependently. The chairpersons reported to the central centennial committee,
and that committee gave assistance when asked. The major concern of the central
planning committee, once activities and chairpersons had been selected, was
to act as an overall coordinator of activities and to plan publicity.

The publication of the centennial book — a handsome hardcover volume of
324 pages entitled *Rexburg, Idaho: The First One Hundred Years* — had both
successes and disappointments. The book was written by Ricks College history
professor David Crowder, who took a one-semester sabbatical to do the research
and writing. Crowder was to receive a nominal fee for writing the book, all
expenses, and 10-percent royalties on sales. The final product is a soundly researched and entertaining book that will serve as a cornerstone for area history
endeavors for years. It is a permanent reminder of the centennial celebration.
The disappointment came when sales were less than hoped for. The committee
printed 5,000 copies of the book, which sold for $13.95. Service clubs loaned
money to pay for printing, and pre-publication sales were made. After nearly
one year, only 2,000 copies had been sold, the service-club loans had not been
repaid, and some expenses were still owed the author. The local population
of 11,500 was about saturated, and were the committee to do a book again it
would print 2,500 copies instead of 5,000.

Gala celebration activities began in March — exactly 100 years after the town's
founding — with the Rexburg Centennial Ball. The ball committee was actually formed and working before the "official" centennial committee was appointed
by the mayor. The Centennial Ball featured two musical groups, a rock band
for younger people and an orchestra for "oldsters"; a reception line of
dignitaries; refreshments; and a lobby area for historical displays. It was held
on the Ricks College campus, the only place in town with a building large

enough to accommodate the 2,000 people who attended. Though the ball was a great success, it was not a money-maker. Still, receipts did cover expenses, and plans are under way to have an annual Rexburg ball.

By far the best-attended event during the celebration was a community musical. *We Can Do It* was a saga of local history, with script and original songs written by a local woman. The play highlighted such events as early homesteading in the area, regional "firsts," the bitter controversy over polygamy, and rebuilding the town after the Teton Dam flood of 1976. The original songs spoke of both good and bad times in Rexburg history and poked good-natured fun at the climate and some of the pioneers. One song, entitled "The Rexburg Wind," noted:

> Jackrabbits by the thousands were an annual plague
> Mosquitoes came a buzzin' round before we learned to spray
> If we had two choices, guess what we would pick?
> Jackrabbits or mosquitoes, cause that wind plumb makes us sick!

The musical, which had a cast of over 250, played for ten nights in the old Tabernacle, with a packed house of 1,000 attending each performance. It received outstanding media publicity and there were numerous ticket outlets in town. In addition, the cast and crew went door to door selling tickets. The musical grossed over $40,000, of which approximately $18,000 were profit. All of those proceeds went to the Tabernacle restoration fund.

The buffalo barbeque, held in August, was organized by the Upper Valley Black Powder Club. With the exception of the buffalo meat, all food and supplies were donated. The uniqueness of the main course assured a large crowd, and people were fed all day. The barbeque was held near the historical society, so many people had an opportunity to visit the museum at the same time. A profit of $2,000 was made and dedicated to the Tabernacle restoration fund.

The biggest disappointment among the major events was the centennial history program, held in late July. David Crowder addressed the audience on the history of Rexburg, but the attendance was quite low. A summer date was set for this activity to coincide with the publication of Crowder's centennial history. In hindsight, the planning committee felt this should have been the first event planned rather than the last. Early in the spring the centennial celebration was a fresh idea, and a local history presentation could have provided a framework and context for the events that followed. By the end of July some people were "celebrated" out. Because of the musical, historical vignettes that aired on local radio, and a series of local history tabloids published by the town newspaper, most people probably felt they knew all they needed to know about Rexburg history by the time of the history program.

In addition to the five major events, the planning committee encouraged other centennial activities based upon existing annual affairs. Thus a Miss Rexburg pageant was reinstituted after a lapse of a few years and was called the Miss

The president of Ricks College spoke at the dedication of that institution's exhibit for the Rexburg Centennial. (Upper Snake River Valley Historical Society)

Rexburg Centennial Contest. Service clubs were encouraged to schedule activities through the centennial committee and to give a centennial theme to annual events like the Lions' Club breakfast. Rexburg has traditionally celebrated "Whoopee Days" around July 4, but in 1983 the activities were bigger than usual and included a 170-mile relay race from Logan, Utah, to Rexburg, commemorating the route taken by early pioneers.

Some organizations also approached the centennial planning committee and asked if there were ways in which they might help with the celebration. One group offered to sponsor a major regional square-dance festival if the committee could provide a $300 loan. The committee did, the festival was a great success, and the loan was repaid.

The committee worked especially hard at publicizing the centennial throughout the region. Beginning in the summer of 1982 a "reunion" was held in each Madison County community. A person in each town was selected as local chairperson, and the reunions followed the same format: someone would give a brief talk on the history of the community, followed by musical entertainment and then reminiscences by old-timers. Not only did these programs instill an interest in local history, they served as reminders of the upcoming

Rexburg centennial. These reunion talks were tape-recorded and made available to people in the communities.

Brochures providing details on centennial activities were produced utilizing an Idaho Travel Council grant and were personally distributed by committee members to motels and chambers of commerce throughout southeastern Idaho. The committee began working early with the local media, and the activities received excellent coverage throughout the celebration. In addition to news stories about all the major events, the newspaper published ten different historical tabloids during the year, and the radio station produced — with the assistance of the department of history at Ricks — a series of historical vignettes. The committee relied almost entirely on free media publicity, though a few radio spots were purchased — at a reduced rate — to advertise the barbeque and play.

In one sense publicity for the Rexburg centennial was easier than for most communities, because the area around the town is so predominantly Mormon. Each church ward has a person who is in charge of informing the congregation of upcoming community events; these spokespersons were amply informed of all centennial activities and passed the word on to their congregations. Even so, in other communities publicity could be enhanced by means of early and regular contacts with local churches.

The committee also relied heavily on word-of-mouth advertising. By utilizing the services of more than 1,000 volunteers who worked on various centennial activities, the value of this type of publicity was considerable. By the time the centennial was over, it is likely that everyone in Madison and neighboring counties knew Rexburg had celebrated.

The Rexburg centennial included a well-rounded mixture of both short-term, "gala" activities — such as the ball, musical, and barbeque — and those with more long-term impact, such as the centennial history. In addition, approximately $20,000 in profits were used to restore the Tabernacle, and other revenues were donated to the historical society. Furthermore, some of the events begun as part of the celebration will become annual activities. Thus, an annual town ball is planned, and the Whoopee Days celebration will be permanently expanded.

The chamber of commerce and various individuals took photographs of centennial events and members of the historical society clipped newspapers. Tapes of all the town "reunions" were made. All of those materials have been deposited at the historical society, with additional copies going to Ricks College. They will serve to permanently document the celebration.

While the Rexburg centennial was a great success, Clements would do some things differently for another celebration. The official centennial committee should have been appointed earlier. Had it not been for the historical society's preliminary planning, the celebration would have been much smaller. With an earlier start there might have been more business support and more funds to work with. The committee would probably have planned a couple of extra major events if it had had a budget or "kitty" to begin with.

There was some confusion between the mayor and the centennial committee. While the mayor believed he was providing guidance, committee members did not feel they were given sufficiently specific instructions. Things might have run more smoothly if the mayor had given the committee a more explicit charge and specific responsibilities.

Finally, it would have been more effective to have had one person in charge of all publicity. While the central committee undertook much publicity, a considerable amount was done by the individual subcommittees as they planned various events. A better method would have been to have one overall publicity coordinator and one press contact person.

THE WALLACE CENTENNIAL, 1984*

"WHEREAS, Colonel W. R. Wallace led a group of prospectors in establishing a town first known as Placer Center, in the heart of the world famous Coeur d'Alene Mining District; and this town's name was later changed to Wallace in honor of its founder; and

"WHEREAS, The City of Wallace grew from its primitive setting in a cedar forest into one of the foremost mining capitals of the world . . .

"NOW, THEREFORE, BE IT RESOLVED by the members . . . of the . . . Idaho Legislature . . . that the members . . . take this opportunity to honor the One Hundredth Anniversary of the founding of the City of Wallace and recognizing its residents, both past and present, for their many memorable achievements."

Wallace, Idaho — a town with about 3,500 residents, "The Silver Capital of the World" — chose to celebrate its 100th anniversary in a highly visible way, including obtaining official state recognition of its centennial. The town is located in the Idaho panhandle and has the only stoplight on Interstate 90 between Seattle and St. Paul. Its residents viewed the centennial celebration as a way of bringing tourists to town while instilling a deeper appreciation of the Silver Valley's history in local residents. Thanks to the dedicated efforts of the Wallace Centennial '84 Committee, both goals were largely met.

Wallace centennial planning started in late summer 1982 when a group of town residents began informally to discuss the upcoming anniversary. In November 1982 Archie Hulsizer, senior vice president of the First National Bank of North Idaho, was appointed by Wallace's mayor as chairman of the Wallace Centennial '84 Committee. The committee included two members of

*Information for this section comes primarily from two interviews with Archie Hulsizer, chairman of the Wallace Centennial '84 Committee. The interviews were conducted in June and December 1984 by Keith Petersen. Additional information came from *Wallace Centennial*, the official 1984 program of the Wallace Centennial '84 Committee.

the city council and had the recognition of the city government, which gave it official status and influence. However, the city government was not involved in the celebration further except to make official proclamations and provide city dignitaries when needed at certain functions. The committee at first consisted of six people and was eventually expanded to eleven. Its members were prominent Wallace residents with connections to the business community and state politicians, as well as to local cultural organizations such as the community museum and library. They had an interest in the town's history and in its economic development, and they had the influence to ensure that the centennial was recognized by the press, business owners, and politicians. They were also hardworking committee members, not mere figureheads. The committee's makeup was largely responsible for the type of high-exposure activities undertaken — and for the success of the celebration.

Chairman Hulsizer stated that the committee functioned with two basic philosophies: first, "If you can't have fun doing a celebration, let's not do it," and second, "Whatever we do, let's do it first class." The committee met regularly twice a month for a one-hour luncheon both before and during the celebration. Its beginning budget was $7,500, contributed by local foundations and individuals. A nonprofit Wallace Centennial Account was established so tax-deductible donations could be made for the celebration. During the course of the celebration the committee raised additional funds at anniversary activities and solicited money from area mining companies. It also received a grant from the Idaho Travel Council to print publicity materials.

While the centennial committee had ample funds to do the "first-class" job desired, its members quickly realized its budget was not sufficient to undertake all of the activities they would like. The committee wanted to have a variety of events, spread over the course of a year. It therefore chose to anchor the centennial celebration on a few key existing organizations and previously planned activities.

For several years District 8 of the Gyro Club — which includes parts of Washington, British Columbia, Alberta, and Idaho — had planned to hold its 1984 annual convention in Wallace to honor that local's 50th anniversary. The Wallace Gyro Club, a civic and social organization, had contributed over $350,000 to various Silver Valley civic causes since its formation in 1934. The annual district convention would bring several hundred visitors to town in July, and the centennial committee decided to capitalize on this ready-made audience and publicity. The Gyro Club's major annual fundraiser — the Lead Creek Derby, which involves estimating the time required for a floating ball to travel down Lead Creek between the towns of Mullan and Wallace — was incorporated as one of the major summertime activities of the centennial.

The Wallace Elks Club traditionally holds an annual Roundup featuring such events as a parade, dance, and banquet. In 1984 this three-day September event

The grand opening of Wallace's centennial celebration included a massive birthday cake decorated with the celebration logo. (Wallace Centennial '84 Committee)

incorporated a centennial theme into its activities and became the key autumn function of the centennial.

Wallace also has a nonprofit Slippery Gulch Association, which was formed in 1946. The Association periodically sponsors Slippery Gulch Days, a gala town celebration geared to making participants feel they are "back in the 'Gay 90's' atmosphere reliving the earlier days of the Wallace mining district." Slippery Gulch Days have traditionally been held to mark significant occasions: the end of World War II; Wallace's Silver Jubilee; the national Bicentennial. Since Archie Hulsizer was president of the Slippery Gulch Association as well as chairman of the centennial committee, the committee had little difficulty convincing the association that 1984 was an appropriate time to have another celebration. Slippery Gulch Days were held from June 21 through June 23, drew an estimated 5,000 visitors to Wallace, and received a heavy amount of regional publicity.

Wallace has also long had an annual town Christmas lighting ceremony. The ceremony in December 1983 served to kick off the town's centennial celebration, while the 1984 ceremony was one of the last official centennial activities.

The committee served as an umbrella organization, encouraging groups to celebrate in their own ways but lending such festivities "official" status, marking them on the community centennial calendar, and thus increasing the variety of events the town was able to undertake as part of its anniversary observance. For example, the 100th anniversary of the Sunshine Mining Company in September was officially recognized as a community centennial activity, but it was entirely planned and financed by the company and was therefore not a drain on the budget or volunteer resources of the centennial committee. Similarly, the United States Forest Service placed an official marker at the site of the Pulaski Tunnel, marking the location of the old mining tunnel that saved the life of Edward Pulaski and thirty-six other fire fighters during the great Idaho forest fire of 1910. The dedication brought dignitaries from throughout the Northwest to Wallace and was made a part of the Wallace Centennial. Members of St. Alphonsus Catholic Church approached the centennial committee about having a St. Alphonsus Day in May to recognize the contributions of the church and its academy to the development of Wallace. Congregation members did all of the planning necessary for the event, but the activity was officially recognized by the centennial committee and became part of the anniversary celebration.

By judiciously utilizing existing committees and events, the Wallace centennial committee was able to "sponsor" many more activities than would have otherwise been possible with its limited budget and personnel. But the committee did undertake some activities that were unique to 1984.

Foremost among these was the opening ceremony in the spring. While centennial activities had been taking place since the previous December, the grand opening came on May 19 with official ceremonies attended by 2,000 people. Among the guests were Idaho's governor and United States senators, north Idaho's congressional representative, city council and county commission members, and state senators and representatives — a tribute to the political clout of the centennial committee members. A Centennial Ball was also held as part of the opening festivities. The ball was open to the entire community and was attended by 250 people — a full house for the limited facilities available.

Among the other activities undertaken or subsidized by the centennial committee as unique events during the anniversary year were a centennial queen pageant; a community play entitled "The First 100 Years"; area block parties at which neighbors gathered for potluck suppers and then congregated downtown for band concerts, singing, and dancing; an "All Class Get-Together" that brought graduates of Wallace High School from all over the country back to town for a reunion; the Wallace Drilling and Mucking Contest, a test of traditional mining skills at which $12,000 in prizes were awarded, attracting contestants from throughout the West; the burying of a time capsule in the courthouse lawn; and a "New Year's Eve 100 Ball," which completed the year's festivities on December 31, 1984.

One of the most successful aspects of the Wallace centennial was the near unanimous participation of the business community. Much of the reason for this success rests with the influence of centennial committee members and their own hard work in seeing that their businesses participated fully. In the spring the committee met with chamber of commerce members and invited town businesses to decorate their shop windows in a historical theme and have workers wear period clothing, if they chose to do so. No one was made to feel uncomfortable if he or she chose not to take part in the festivities. Awards were given for the best windows and best dress. During the summer of 1984 virtually every Wallace store window was "historically" decorated. Many businesses also decorated their buildings with bunting and flags. It was impossible to drive through town without knowing something special was happening, and most businesses reported a substantial increase in revenues over previous years. In fact, the centennial actually brought some new businesses to town, and during 1984 virtually every commercial space in the community was occupied. In December many of the businesses decorated their windows with historic Christmas themes.

The Wallace centennial was characterized by an abundance of top-quality publicity. It would have been virtually impossible to live in the Wallace region in 1984 and not hear about the anniversary. In fact, some of the publicity was national, such as when ABC Television's "Good Morning America" program televised parts of the opening ceremonies. Spokane television and radio stations and virtually all regional newspapers devoted a considerable amount of attention to the celebration during the year. The committee hired a professional advertising and design firm to handle most publicity. This firm was responsible for making contacts with the press and for producing the many professional-quality advertising materials that helped spread the word of the centennial. Included among these materials were 9,000 pocket calendars, several thousand placemats used in area restaurants, publicity flyers in motels, and 5,000 forty-page programs, subsidized by advertising, that gave a brief background of Wallace history and described the centennial activities. The publicity firm also developed an official logo, a caricature of a prospector and his mule; chose a picture of the Wallace train depot — which is on the National Register of Historic Places — as the official centennial photograph; and developed the celebration theme, "Celebrating 100 Years of Wallace Mining History." The logo, photograph, and theme were used extensively on all publicity materials. In fact, the centennial committee allowed anyone to use these items free of charge, believing that the more they were used, the more the community would benefit. Several businesses had cups, plates, and other souvenirs printed with the logo.

The centennial committee worked on other forms of publicity as well. Centennial pins were produced and sold by the Elks Youth Activity Association as a

A centennial parade was one of many ways in which Wallace celebrated. (Wallace Centennial '84 Committee)

fundraiser. Bumper stickers and stickers for envelopes were produced. The committee obtained post office box number 100, which served to remind correspondents of the significance of 1984. All people over 80 years old who had lived in the community at least 50 years were named "Honorary Centennial Chairpeople," received free tickets to all events, and had their biographies published in the local newspaper. The newspaper published a special centennial supplement in the spring and another at the end of the year that highlighted the events of 1984. The committee sponsored a centennial art contest and printed the winning entry on a handsome centennial poster.

It was not the purpose of the committee to make money from the centennial, other than what was needed to help advertise events and sponsor programs. Thus it was willing to allow free use of the logo and charged only a break-even admission to some events and no admission to others. In addition to requesting and receiving contributions from area foundations and the Idaho Travel Council, its major fundraising activity was the minting of a silver commemorative coin. The front of the coin presented an engraving of early-day Wallace, and the back noted the centennial dates. The committee minted 8,500 of the coins, which it sold for $22.50 each. Sales were assisted when area mining companies distributed flyers about the coin in their annual reports to stockholders. By the end of 1984 the committee expected that the coin project would be profitable.

The Wallace centennial committee was smaller than many town centennial groups. It succeeded primarily because its members were hardworking, had influence in the community, and did not attempt to take on more activities than they could complete in a "first-class" manner. The committee did sponsor a number of events itself, but these were spread evenly over the course of the year, not only to prevent committee members from being overburdened but also to ensure that the community would not tire of the celebration. The majority of Wallace's centennial activities were planned and sponsored by other groups. The success of the celebration lay in the ability of its centennial committee to give its "official" blessing to such events, helping with advertising and occasionally with funding, but allowing other groups to celebrate in their own ways without interference and without draining the central committee of its limited volunteer resources. Because of the influence of its members, the committee also had access to more funds than many small-town anniversary committees do. When money was needed to sponsor or advertise an activity, it was available. The result was an outstanding publicity program that assured high attendance at events.

Hulsizer felt that one of the key roles the committee played was to serve as a central coordinating body that established event dates to prevent conflicts. It also made sure there were plenty of motel rooms available on the days needed, and it advertised activities. Even though many small committees and organizations actually participated in the event, having a central steering committee was indispensable. Hulsizer also attributed the success of the celebration to the dedication of the centennial committee members: "You need to have good, hard-working people to make it happen. An 'interest' just isn't enough."

The Wallace centennial did not produce any items traditionally thought of as having a long-lasting impact, such as the publication of a history book or the completion of an oral history project. The committee did commission a photographer to document centennial activities, and these photographs will be permanently retained in the community. In several intangible ways, though, the centennial will have long-lasting significance. Many businesses took this opportunity to clean and refurbish their buildings, and virtually all business owners saw the important role history can play in increasing tourism — which could well lead to more marketing activities with historical themes in the future. And, just as 1984 began with an official mayoral proclamation designating it as the centennial year, so did 1985 begin with an official mayoral proclamation designating it as "Wallace — 100 Plus 1." The centennial committee plans to continue meeting to help centralize publicity for community events, and several activities undertaken for the centennial, such as the block parties and the drilling and mucking contest, may become annual activities. The Wallace centennial was eminently successful in bringing about a community cohesiveness and demonstrating that history is marketable and can be profitable. It created an enormous amount of enthusiasm, and there is reason to believe this enthusiasm will translate into long-lasting community benefits.

THE JEROME DIAMOND JUBILEE, 1982*

Jerome, a southern Idaho town of about 7,500 people, was desert land until the Twin Falls North Side Land and Water Company built reservoirs and canals in the Magic Valley. Water first began flowing in the company's canal systems in 1908, and since that time the area has become a rich agricultural region. The city of Jerome was platted in the summer of 1907, and the first town lots were sold in the fall of that year. In 1982 Jerome residents celebrated their diamond jubilee. In many ways, though, theirs was more than just a town celebration, for residents from throughout Jerome County and the Magic Valley participated in the anniversary observance.

The Jerome diamond jubilee was unique in several ways. No formal central planning committee was appointed. There was no central treasury, and no fundraising was undertaken. Yet, because of the enthusiasm and energy of the coordinators, the celebration was highly successful and attracted thousands of people to various anniversary events.

Planning for the diamond jubilee began in July 1981 when the Jerome Chamber of Commerce sent letters to organizations and individuals throughout the county inviting them to a brainstorming and planning meeting. The meeting was well attended, and from those present a volunteer "core group" emerged that functioned as the central planning committee, although it was never officially designated as such. This central committee consisted of approximately twenty people, including representatives from service and social clubs, businesses, schools, churches, the local media, and city and county law-enforcement offices. The committee met monthly, eventually changing this schedule so as to meet every two weeks and then once a week as the time for celebration approached. Ethel Nelson, secretary for the chamber of commerce, served as the unofficial committee coordinator, calling meetings, taking minutes, and doing mailings. She had the complete support and backing of the chamber for her many anniversary-celebration tasks.

The committee decided at the first planning meeting in July to concentrate the celebration into a two-week period in August 1982, anchored on the Jerome County Fair and the Jerome community parade, traditionally the best-attended annual events in the county. It also decided to incorporate other annual events into the celebration and to invite groups and organizations to sponsor special

*Information for this sketch comes primarily from an interview with Virginia Ricketts of the Jerome Diamond Jubilee Committee, conducted by Madeline Buckendorf in January 1985. Additional information comes from *The History of the North Side*, a supplement to the *North Side News* of August 5, 1982, written by Ricketts.

events for the diamond jubilee if they so chose. The committee put no pressure on any group to participate in the celebration, but if one wanted to sponsor a special activity or give a historic theme to a previously scheduled event, the committee offered help in coordinating activities to prevent conflicts. The committee also decided that it would not sponsor any events itself but would instead serve as a central coordinating, idea, and assistive body. Committee members decided there would be no need for fundraising since each organization would be in charge of planning, implementing, and paying for its own activities.

After the initial brainstorming session, organizational representatives went back to their individual groups to discuss the ideas presented. The response of Jerome County organizations was enthusiastic and positive. In fact, so many groups were interested in participating that it proved impossible to consolidate all activities into a two-week period.

Organizational representatives brought word of this enthusiastic response back to the second meeting of the central planning committee. It was at this time that the central committee started filling its vital role as the overall coordinating unit by developing a community calendar of anniversary events. Each organization was given the opportunity to suggest an activity it wanted to sponsor and when it wanted the event held. The central committee then filled in the calendar, avoiding conflicts so that each event would receive the full attention of the community. This community planning calendar proved vital to the celebration's success.

Besides serving as a coordinating body, the central committee also took responsibility for publicizing the diamond jubilee. One of the first committee tasks was sponsoring community contests for an anniversary theme and logo, with the chamber of commerce offering prize money. The theme contest was won by the editor of the local newspaper — who contributed the money back to the committee — with the entry "The North Side . . . A Cause for Pride." The central committee requested that all organizations planning anniversary activities adhere to this theme. Since the theme was broad enough to be widely interpreted, groups had little difficulty incorporating it.

The logo contest was also a community-wide event and helped to stir enthusiasm and interest. A local high-school student won the contest by submitting an entry emphasizing the county's agricultural and railroad history. The theme was then incorporated into the logo, and the central committee encouraged the widest possible use of this anniversary symbol. It was used extensively by the media and by many organizations that put it on stationery. The central committee insisted upon only one use restriction, that no group or business be allowed to use the logo to make money for itself. Other than that, logo use was free and encouraged. As a result, the logo became widely disseminated, and county residents began to associate it with the upcoming celebration.

Above: *Among the community-wide events included in Jerome's diamond jubilee was an antique and classic car show.* Below: *Jerome Boy Scouts helped with parking and served as color guard and tour assistants during the diamond-jubilee tour of the Idaho Power Company's plant at Shoshone Falls. (Both, Jerome County Historical Society)*

The central planning committee next approached a local printing business about the possibility of making placemats for the celebration. The printing concern agreed to donate placemats to all area restaurants, and committee member Don Sparhawk donated time to design them. The placemats included a historical map of Jerome County and, below the anniversary theme, had a calendar of events. The placemats were also widely disseminated and generated interest in the celebration. Committee member Virginia Ricketts wrote a series of newspaper articles on the history of the area and took slide programs to organizations, schools, and churches. These activities, too, helped to create an anniversary atmosphere.

The early and active participation of media representatives provided an element vital to the success of the Jerome diamond jubilee. Area radio, television, and newspaper outlets sent representatives to the first planning meeting, and most of these people became permanent members of the central planning committee. These media representatives did not have to be asked to help publicize events. They came up with their own promotional ideas and coordinated all advertising needed to sponsor special publicity items. For example, the Jerome weekly newspaper printed special daily editions during the main week of the celebration that listed upcoming events and highlighted the previous day's activities. The paper also published a special sixty-eight-page historical supplement. The local radio station sponsored a local history trivia contest and awarded prizes to winners. The program was so popular that it has been continued. The Twin Falls television station aired a special half-hour program about the celebration, funded by four Jerome sponsors, one week before the event. In fact, Virginia Ricketts felt that the success of the celebration was directly attributable to inviting the media to the first planning meeting and encouraging them to participate actively as permanent members of the central committee. "That was the biggest plus we had," she noted.

While the central committee decided to highlight the two weeks in August surrounding the county fair as the major time of celebration, it also invited groups that normally sponsored annual events to adhere to the anniversary theme and make their activities a part of the celebration as well. Thus the first anniversary activity was Jerome Farmers' Night, held in March. This event is sponsored annually by the chamber of commerce as a gesture of appreciation for area farmers. In 1982 it took on a historical theme as the oldest farmers still living on the North Side tract were honored. Other annual events, such as the North Side Players' presentation and the high-school rodeo, similarly followed the anniversary theme.

Other groups and organizations chose to sponsor special events during the main celebration in August. Jerome merchants were among the most enthusiastic anniversary supporters. They sponsored a special moonlight sale, had historical displays in store windows, and contributed money to other organizations. For example, the Jerome County Historical Society sponsored a North Side Gallery as one of its major diamond jubilee activities. After recruiting historic photographs from present and former community residents, society members selected 100 of these to be enlarged and displayed in a special exhibit. Area merchants and professional offices contributed $10 to have historic photographs enlarged, then were allowed to keep the enlargements at the close of the exhibit.

Churches also actively participated. Many provided free publicity for upcoming celebration events. Some area churches also combined for a joint observance of the first tent religious service held in Jerome. Four congregations cooperated with the historical society in hosting a tour of four of the older church buildings in town. Since the main celebration was in the summer, schools did not participate quite as actively. However, they did allow use of their facilities for many events and hosted an alumni football game and cross-country race in August.

Civic clubs and service organizations likewise participated in the festivities. The Kiwanis Club sponsored a fun run; the Rotary had a barbeque; the Lions held a breakfast and dinner and sponsored the first annual Miss North Side Pageant. The Senior Citizens' Club sponsored a reunion breakfast, inviting former residents back to town for the celebration. Many groups and businesses had floats in the community parade, and several also helped to fund the large fireworks display that served to officially end activities on August 22.

Two of the area's most important businesses sponsored two of the most popular events. The North Side Canal Company sponsored a tour of the North Side Canal System — the first public tour of the system since the canals were built. The Idaho Power Company sponsored an open house and guided tours of its Shoshone Falls power plant and published a brochure on the plant. These voluntary tours were indicative of the enthusiastic support area businesses gave the celebration.

As with any large, multifaceted activity, not every project was a complete success. For example, the chamber of commerce's T-shirt and cap sales did not do as well as the chamber had expected. Some members of the central planning committee had hoped to republish one of the original brochures promoting the North Side country, but financing for such a venture was not available. Nonetheless, as Ricketts remarked, "The celebration was much more successful than probably we ever dreamed it would be."

Despite the committee's inability to republish the historic promotional brochure, the celebration did have long-lasting impact. Much original historical research was undertaken and made accessible to the public in the special newspaper tabloid, *The History of the North Side*. The historical society printed a very successful diamond jubilee calendar. The calendars were priced at $3.50,

1,500 copies were printed, and marketing began in November 1981. The society also gathered over 800 local historic photographs by contacting present and past area residents. These were all copied and are now a part of the society's permanent research collection. The enthusiasm generated by the celebration has also brought long-lasting community benefits. For example, Jerome now has a special "Celebration Weekend" preceding the county fair each year and has repeated many of the successful activities from the diamond jubilee, such as the Senior Citizens' breakfast, street dance, Miss North Side Pageant, Northwest Regional Antique Car Show, and arts and crafts show. Further, the county historical society has directly benefited from the enthusiasm generated by the celebration, as there is now much local support for the development of a community museum. As Virginia Ricketts remarked, the best long-lasting effect of the diamond jubilee was that people "found out that they can do something that turned out big, and do it well."

Ricketts felt there were several keys to the celebration's success. One was that planning began a year in advance. While it is essential to begin this early, she cautions groups about beginning too early because interest can lag and the planning group might lose momentum. The size of the community and the types of projects to be undertaken will determine when planning should begin.

Another key element of the Jerome anniversary celebration was the broad-based nature of the central planning committee. For example, media representation was essential. Equally helpful was representation from city and county law-enforcement offices. When the central committee began planning for a street dance at the town's main intersection, law officers told them this was impossible because of interference with traffic on a state highway and then worked with the committee to find an equally suitable location.

"I can't think of a thing that I would change," remarked Ricketts, and others in Jerome would agree. For example, area merchants met after the celebration, agreed it had been a success, and were largely responsible for seeing that the annual "Celebration Weekend" continued. The chamber of commerce helped provide the minimal financing the central planning committee needed and willingly provided the coordination services of secretary Ethel Nelson. In a technical sense, the chamber might have "lost" money on the celebration, but chamber members agreed that the expense was well worth it in terms of generating community enthusiasm and a considerable amount of revenue for Jerome businesses.

Appendix A

Sources of Technical Assistance

NATIONAL

American Association for State and Local History
172 Second Ave. N., Suite 102
Nashville, Tennessee 37201
>   AASLH is the single most important organization for people working in local history. As can be seen in this handbook's bibliography, it has published numerous helpful books and technical leaflets. *History News,* a bimonthly journal, and *History News Dispatch,* a monthly newsletter, are sent to all members. AASLH also offers workshops, seminars, independent-study courses, consultant services, and an annual meeting that includes sessions with technical and practical information.

American Association of Museums
1055 Thomas Jefferson St., N.W.
Washington, D.C. 20007
>   AAM was founded in 1906 and is the largest museum organization in the United States. Unfortunately, in recent years it has become an organization of value primarily to large art museums. It publishes *Museum News,* a bimonthly magazine; *Aviso,* a monthly newsletter; and several useful books.

American Association of Youth Museums
Corpus Christi Museum
1919 North Water
Corpus Christi, Texas 78401

American Library Association
50 East Huron St.
Chicago, Illinois 60611
>   The ALA offers helpful publications, consulting services, and an annual conference.

Association for Living Historical Farms and Agricultural Museums
Smithsonian Institution
Washington, D.C. 20560

> The association, founded in 1970, maintains a large information bank providing a central repository of information on plants, animals, tools, and implements used in American agriculture in the past.

Canadian Museums Association
331 Cooper St., Suite 400
Ottawa, Ontario, CANADA K2P 0G5

> The association offers useful publications and technical assistance.

Canadian Oral History Association
P.O. Box 301, Station A
Ottawa, Ontario, CANADA K1N 8V3

> COHA sponsors an annual conference and publishes an annual *Journal* that contains articles of interest to people in the field.

Center for Community Economic Development
1320 — 19th St., N.W.
Washington, D.C. 20036

> The center's primary function is to conduct research on community development corporations and other community-based economic organizations. It acts as a clearinghouse for material on community economic development and provides technical assistance to community groups regarding incorporation and bylaws, organizing strategies, fundraising and proposal writing, and board training.

The Foundation Center
888 Seventh Ave.
New York, N.Y. 10019

> The center is a national service organization supported by foundations to provide information on foundation giving. It helps grant-seekers determine which of the 22,000 active United States foundations may be most interested in their project. The Center publishes reference books on foundations and also has a national network of cooperating libraries — at least one in each state — that provide free access to all of the center's books, plus a wide range of other books, periodicals, and documents related to foundations and philanthropy.

Institute of Museum Services
Washington, D.C. 20506

> IMS was established by Congress in 1976 to assist museums in modernizing methods and facilities. The Institute offers grants to museums in

a number of programs. It is the only federal agency to award general operating support funds for museums.

Library of Congress
Washington, D.C. 20540

The library offers reference and consultation services in the fields of preservation, restoration, and protection of library materials. It will answer brief technical inquiries at no charge.

Museum Reference Center
Office of Museum Programs
Room 2235 Arts and Industries Bldg.
Smithsonian Institution
Washington, D.C. 20560

The center was established in 1974 as a resource for museum personnel and researchers. It maintains a collection of technical literature about museum operations, and it disseminates bibliographies and information on specific museum issues.

National Endowment for the Arts
Washington, D.C. 20506

The NEA, a federal agency, awards grants to promote the arts in a wide number of areas, including folk arts, architecture, literature, music, and museums.

National Endowment for the Humanities
Washington, D.C. 20506

The NEH is a federal agency founded in 1965 to support research, education, and public activity in the humanities. The endowment offers matching grants in a number of different programs of interest to people involved in local history work.

National Historical Publications and Records Commission
National Archives
Washington, D.C. 20408

The NHPRC, a federal agency, awards grants to improve archival programs and to assist in the cataloging and preserving of significant manuscript collections.

National History Day, Inc.
11201 Euclid Ave.
Cleveland, Ohio 44106

Like its better-known counterpart, Science Fair, National History Day encourages school children to undertake projects. NHD provides a national theme each year. Students participate on a district level with winners eventually advancing to state and national competitions. More than thirty states are presently participating in National History Day.

National Main Street Center
1785 Massachusetts Ave., N.W.
Washington, D.C. 20036
A division of the National Trust for Historic Preservation, the NMSC was organized to promote the use of historic preservation concepts in downtown revitalization efforts. Publications, case studies, training, and other activities are available.

National Register of Historic Places
National Park Service
Washington, D.C. 20240

National Trust for Historic Preservation
1785 Massachusetts Ave., N.W
Washington, D.C. 20036
A private organization chartered by Congress to facilitate public participation in historic preservation, the Trust sponsors conferences, seminars, and workshops; provides low-interest loans, matching grants, and consultants; and publishes many useful books and booklets. Members receive *Preservation News*, a monthly newspaper, and *Historic Preservation*, a bimonthly magazine.

Newberry Library
60 W. Walton St.
Chicago, Illinois 60610
The Newberry Library offers bibliographies, workshops, and seminars in a wide variety of areas of interest to people working in local and family history. However, workshops and seminars are generally open only to scholars.

Oral History Association
P.O. Box 926, University Station
Lexington, KY 40506-0025
OHA publishes a quarterly, *Oral History Newsletter,* which describes new developments in the field. It also publishes the annual *Oral History Review* and sponsors an annual colloquium and workshop.

Preservation Action
1700 Connecticut Ave., N.W., Suite 400
Washington, D.C. 20009
A national lobby organized to ensure that preservation issues are heard in Congress, Preservation Action holds an annual conference and

publishes a newsletter, *Alert,* to keep members up to date on government appropriations for preservation.

Public Interest Public Relations, Inc.
225 W. 34th St.
New York, N.Y. 10001
PIPR helps nonprofit groups communicate with their audiences. Its goals are to help develop fundraising programs; assist in the creation of informational materials such as annual reports, brochures, and newsletters; generate publicity in the print and broadcast media; and advise on the organization of special events.

Regional Conference of Historical Agencies
314 E. Seneca St.
Manlius, N.Y. 13104
RCHA publishes inexpensive technical information sheets of special usefulness to those affiliated with museums and historical societies. RCHA will mail a list of information sheets available.

Smithsonian Institution
Washington, D.C. 20560
The Smithsonian offers many services, programs, and publications useful to people involved in museum and local history work.

Society of American Archivists
600 S. Federal, Suite 504
Chicago, Illinois 60605
The SAA is a professional association of individuals and institutions interested in the preservation and use of archives, manuscripts, sound recordings, photographs, films, and maps. The Society publishes numerous helpful books and pamphlets and offers archival workshops. Members receive *American Archivist,* its quarterly journal, and a newsletter. The annual meeting includes sessions providing practical information.

State Arts Committees or Councils
In each state
Each state has a state arts committee or council that is funded by the National Endowment for the Arts as well as by private contributions and sometimes the state government. The committees are service and funding organizations. They can offer professional technical assistance and matching grants for arts-related projects, often including folk arts.

State Historic Preservation Offices
In each state
> The SHPO in each state is responsible for its state's overall historic preservation plan; administers federal preservation grants for survey, planning, and protection; nominates properties to the National Register of Historic Places; conducts surveys and inventories; and provides technical assistance to communities and individuals.

State Humanities Committees
In each state
> Each state has a state humanities committee funded by the National Endowment for the Humanities as well as by private contributions and sometimes the state government. The committees can offer professional assistance and matching grants for humanities-related projects.

Superintendent of Documents
U.S. Government Printing Office
Washington, D.C. 20402
> The Government Printing Office prints thousands of books and pamphlets on any number of topics. Write for a listing of publications available.

Technical Preservation Services Division
National Park Service
Washington, D.C. 20240

IDAHO
Note: While only Idaho sources are listed, similar agencies and organizations are available in each state.

Association for the Humanities in Idaho (state humanities committee)
650 W. State St., Room 300
Boise, ID 83702

Department of Commerce
Statehouse
Boise, ID 83720

Foundation Center Library
Caldwell Public Library
1010 Dearborn St.
Caldwell, ID 83605

Idaho Association of Museums
c/o The Herrett Museum
College of Southern Idaho
Box 1238
Twin Falls, ID 83301

Idaho Commission on the Arts
304 W. State St.
Boise, ID 83720
[includes Folk Arts Program]

Idaho Historic Preservation Council
P.O. Box 1495
Boise, ID 83701

Idaho State Historical Society
610 N. Julia Davis Dr.
Boise, ID 83702
    Divisions:
        Historical Library
        Idaho Genealogical Library
        Idaho Oral History Center
        Idaho State Historic Preservation Office
        State Museum
        Old Idaho Penitentiary

Idaho State Library
325 West State St.
Boise, ID 83702

Idaho Travel Council
Statehouse
Boise, ID 83720

Snake River Regional Studies Center
College of Idaho
Caldwell, ID 83605

Universities and colleges
(These institutions have people with expertise, libraries, and numerous other
resources useful for local project planners.)

Appendix B

Publicity Materials

NEWS RELEASE

For release: IMMEDIATELY   Contact: John Doe

Doe County Historical Society

P.O. Box 100

Doe, ID 83333

575-6210

DOE HISTORICAL SOCIETY TO SPONSOR PRESERVATION WORKSHOP

The Doe County Historical Society will sponsor a regional workshop on historic preservation on Saturday, July 14, 1986, at the McWilliams History Center, 111 S. Jefferson Street, Doe, Idaho. The conference is free and open to the public and is partially funded by a grant from the Idaho State Historic Preservation Office.

Among topics to be discussed are tax incentives for historic preservation; what it means to be listed on the National Register of Historic Places; grass-roots

— more —

Preservation Workshop — 2

involvement in historic preservation; and how historic preservation can aid the

economy of Doe. State and regional experts will address these and other topics

and will be accessible all day to answer questions.

This conference is especially geared to business people, government officials,

owners of older buildings, and all those interested in preserving Doe's architec-

tural heritage. This is the first time a conference of this type has been held

in the Doe area, and it offers an opportunity for local people to learn more

about historic preservation.

The conference schedule follows:

9:00-9:30 a.m.: Registration with coffee and donuts.

9:30-10:45 a.m.: "The National Register of Historic Places: Concept and

Misconceptions." Tom Jones, Pacific Northwest Regional Office, National Park

Service.

10:45-11:00: Break.

11:00 a.m.-noon: "Historic Preservation and Community Rehabilitation:

A Role for Everyone." Sally Smith, Western Regional Office, National Trust

for Historic Preservation.

Noon-1:30: Catered lunch.

— more —

Preservation Workshop — 3

1:30-2:30: "Tax Incentives for Historic Preservation." Jessie Johnson,

Johnson and Associates, Business Consultants, Boise.

2:30-2:45: Break.

2:45-3:45: "How Historic Preservation Can Aid the Economy of Doe."

William Jones, Idaho State Historic Preservation Officer.

3:45-5:00: Questions and comments.

5:00-: No-host cocktail hour with an opportunity to discuss individual con-

cerns with speakers.

Those wanting more information on this free conference should contact John

Doe at the Doe County Historical Society, 575-6210.

#

Release date: July 1, 1986

Points to note about the news release:
— Date the material can be used by news media is at the top. (Usually material
is for "immediate" release. You cannot allow one news outlet to run information before another.)
— A contact person, address, and telephone number are provided at the top.
— A suggested headline is provided. Most newspapers will write their own
headlines, but you should always suggest one that incorporates what you consider to be the most important message in the release.
— White space is allowed on top, wide margins are used, and the release
is double-spaced. This allows for editorial comments, changes, and additions
by the newspaper.
— The release is concise but includes all essential information, including
names. A cover letter could accompany the release, inviting a reporter to call

the contact person in case the newspaper decides to run a larger story and needs further information.
— The most essential information is placed in the first paragraph.
— The last paragraph contains information on how readers can obtain more information.
— A "#" mark signifies that this is the last page of the release ("30" can also be used). The word "-more-" is used at the end of each page except the last one to signify that the release continues. Also note that each page after the first is numbered at the top, preceded by a short heading describing the activity outlined in the release. This helps the reporter keep news releases together despite an oftentimes jumbled desk.
— A release date is provided. This is not essential if the heading provides an actual date, but if the word "immediately" is used a specific date should be included so that the newspaper knows the material is timely.

SAMPLE PUBLIC SERVICE ANNOUNCEMENT

PUBLIC SERVICE ANNOUNCEMENT

Good: July 5—13, 1986   Contact: John Doe

Doe County Historical Society

P.O. Box 100

Doe, ID 83333

575-6210

THE DOE COUNTY HISTORICAL SOCIETY WILL SPONSOR A

REGIONAL WORKSHOP ON HISTORIC PRESERVATION ON SATURDAY

— more —

Preservation Workshop — 2

JULY 14, 1986, AT THE McWILLIAMS HISTORY CENTER, 111 SOUTH

JEFFERSON STREET, DOE. THE CONFERENCE IS FREE AND OPEN

TO THE PUBLIC AND WILL RUN FROM 9:00 A.M. TO 5:00 P.M.

SPEAKERS WILL ADDRESS SUCH TOPICS AS TAX INCENTIVES FOR

HISTORIC PRESERVATION AND HOW PRESERVATION CAN AID THE

ECONOMY OF DOE. THIS IS THE FIRST CONFERENCE OF ITS TYPE

TO BE HELD IN THE DOE AREA. FOR FURTHER INFORMATION CON-

TACT JOHN DOE AT THE DOE COUNTY HISTORICAL SOCIETY,

575-6210.

#

Points to note about the public service announcement:
— The dates the announcement should be aired are provided at the top.
— A contact person, address, and telephone number are provided at the top.
— The message is kept short and does not utilize complex sentences or words that are difficult to read over the air (try reading your own PSA's out loud). The message is typed in all capitals, double spaced, for easier reading on the air.
— The last sentence in the announcement contains information on how listeners can obtain more information.
— A "#" mark signifies that this is the end of the announcement ("30" can also be used).

Bibliography

The following is not a comprehensive bibliography but is intended to provide basic information in a number of areas. In most cases, the publications cited have bibliographies that will lead readers to other materials in the field.

The notation "AASLH" in the following citations refers to the American Association for State and Local History, 172 Second Avenue N., Nashville, Tennessee 37201.

Several of these publications are now out of print; interested parties should try inter-library loan to obtain copies. Most recent materials can usually be purchased directly from the publisher.

ANNIVERSARY CELEBRATIONS — GENERAL

Celebrate! '89. Olympia: Washington Centennial Commission, 1983-.

>This regular publication of the Washington Centennial Commission contains helpful hints from local committees that are planning for the state's centennial in 1989, as well as advice and tips from the Commission. [Subscriptions are free upon written request. Contact Washington Centennial Commission, 111 West 21st Ave., Olympia, Washington 98504, Mailstop KL-12.]

Centennial Guide for Local Committees. Raleigh: North Carolina Confederate Centennial Commission, 1960.

>Some good basic hints for grass-roots committees. Written for the centennial celebration of the Civil War, but helpful for all anniversary commemorations. [Out of print.]

Crouch, Tom D. *Ohio Bicentennial Guide: Suggestions for Commemorating the American Revolution Bicentennial*. Columbus: Ohio Historical Center, 1973.

>Many helpful hints for planning anniversary celebrations, ranging from cookbooks to historic-house tours to restoration projects. [Out of print.]

Dunn, Walter S., Jr. *Local Historical Celebrations*. Information Sheet No. 20. Manlius, N.Y.: Regional Conference of Historical Agencies, [1975?].

Only two pages long, but filled with excellent ideas for grass-roots celebrations. [Available from the Regional Conference of Historical Agencies, 314 E. Seneca St., Manlius, N.Y. 13104.]

Galveston. Texas Commission on the Arts and Humanities; Washington, D.C.: American Revolution Bicentennial Administration, 1973. *Tacoma.* Olympia: Washington Arts Commission; Washington, D.C.: American Revolution Bicentennial Administration, 1974. *Quincy.* Washington, D.C.: American Revolution Bicentennial Administration, 1974.

These three booklets outline activities in three cities, all pilot projects done on contract with the ARBC. Good information on project ideas at the local level, fundraising, publicity. [Out of print.]

Hartje, Robert G. *Bicentennial USA: Pathways to Celebration.* Nashville: AASLH, 1973.

Unfortunately, this book is not as helpful as it could have been. The bulk of it is devoted to detailing how other states and provinces have celebrated anniversaries in the past. This makes for somewhat interesting reading, but not for an indispensible planning guide for grassroots organizers. There are two helpful chapters on planning and project ideas.

The Report of the British Columbia Centennial Committee. Victoria: The Committee, 1959.

Very good for project ideas. [Out of print.]

Report of the South Carolina Tricentennial Commission. Columbia: The Commission, 1971.

Includes an excellent section of reports on county celebrations with many local project ideas. Also good sections on school projects and on scholarly and religious activities. [Out of print.]

Sivesind, Raymond S. *How to Organize a Centennial Celebration.* Bulletin No. 100. Madison: State Historical Society of Wisconsin, 1956.

Although only fourteen pages long and a bit out of date, this is one of the few guides of its kind and contains some helpful grass-roots hints. [Out of print.]

Snake River Echoes [quarterly publication of the Upper Snake River Valley Historical Society].

Vol. 12, No. 1 and Vol. 12, No. 4 provide some good practical tips on how Rexburg successfully celebrated its anniversary in 1983. [Available from the Society, P.O. Box 244, Rexburg, Idaho 83440].

FUNDRAISING

Alderson, William T., Jr. *Securing Grant Support: Effective Planning and Preparation.* Technical Leaflet No. 62. Nashville: AASLH, 1972.

Good basic information for beginning grant-writers, with a helpful checklist and bibliography. [Out of print.]

Alter, JoAnne. "101 Surefire Fundraising Ideas," *Family Circle,* October 1976.

Some good grass-roots ideas. [Available from Reprint Dept., Family Circle, 488 Madison Ave., New York, N.Y. 10022.]

Brownrigg, W. Grant. *Corporate Fundraising: A Practical Plan of Action.* New York: American Council for the Arts, 1979.

Describes practical approaches to soliciting contributions from businesses. [Available from the American Council for the Arts, 570 Seventh Ave., New York, N.Y. 10018.]

Coe, Linda C., ed. *Cultural Directory II: Federal Funds and Services for the Arts and Humanities.* Washington, D.C.: Smithsonian Institution Press, 1980.

A good companion to the Hartman book listed below. Provides an introduction to sources of federal assistance for cultural activities. Contains 200 entries with information on what and for whom assistance is available, comments, and contacts for further information.

Des Marais, Philip. *How to Get Government Grants.* Hartsdale, N.Y.: Public Service Materials Center, 1980.

This book, utilizing many case histories, explains how to carry out a program for obtaining government grants. [Available from Public Service Materials Center, 111 North Central Ave., Hartsdale, N.Y. 10530.]

Flanagan, Joan. *The Grass Roots Fundraising Book: How to Raise Money in Your Community.* Chicago: Swallow Press, 1977.

Perhaps the best local, grass-roots fundraising guide available. Includes everything from membership drives to bake sales. [Available from the Youth Project, 1000 Wisconsin Ave., N.W., Washington, D.C. 20007.]

Hartman, Hedy A., comp. *Funding Sources and Technical Assistance for Museums and Historical Agencies: A Guide to Public Programs.* Nashville: AASLH, 1979.

Though somewhat outdated because of rapid changes in federal agencies, this is still an indispensable guide.

Heywood, Ann M. *The Resource Directory for Funding and Managing Non-profit Organizations.* New York, N.Y.: Edna McConnell Clark Foundation, 1982.

One of the best annotated bibliographies of fundraising available. Also contains addresses of key organizations that can offer technical assistance to nonprofits. [One free copy per nonprofit organization is available from the Edna McConnell Clark Foundation, 250 Park Ave., New York, N.Y. 10017.]

Hillman, Howard, and Karen Abarbanel. *The Art of Winning Foundation Grants.* Hartsdale, N.Y.: Public Service Materials Center, [periodically updated].

Of the several books providing hints for writing foundation grants, this is one of the least expensive. It covers initial research, deciding upon a foundation to approach, appointments, and writing a proposal. [Available from Public Service Materials Center, 111 N. Central Ave., Hartsdale, N.Y. 10530.]

How to Apply for and Retain Exempt Status for Your Organization. Internal Revenue Service, Publication No. 557. Washington, D.C.: Government Printing Office, [periodically updated].

Jacquette, F. Lee, and Barbara I. Jacquette. *What Makes a Good Proposal.* New York: The Foundation Center, 1973.

Short brochure offers tips on how to write a foundation proposal. [One free copy available from The Foundation Center, 888 Seventh Ave., New York, N.Y. 10019.]

Mayer, Robert A. *What Will a Foundation Look for When You Submit a Grant Proposal.* New York: The Foundation Center, 1972.

[One free copy available from The Foundation Center, 888 Seventh Ave., New York, N.Y. 10019.]

Private Funds for Historic Preservation. Washington, D.C.: National Trust for Historic Preservation, 1979.

Fundraising planning, developing a fundraising calendar, soliciting assistance, and sources of private support are among the topics covered.

Public Funds for Historic Preservation. Washington, D.C.: National Trust for Historic Preservation, 1977, 1983.

A concise guide to federal funds available, with a few tips on state and local funding.

Recruiting Volunteers: Views, Techniques, and Comments. Washington, D.C.: National Center for Voluntary Action, 1976.

[Available from National Center for Voluntary Action, 1785 Massachusetts Ave., N.W., Washington, D.C., 20036.]

PUBLICATIONS TO HELP WITH VARIOUS PROJECTS

Researching and writing local history

Allen, Barbara, and Lynwood Montell. *From Memory to History: Using Oral Sources in Local Historical Research.* Nashville: AASLH, 1981.

This book goes beyond most oral history guidebooks to discuss some of the theoretical considerations of oral history.

Austin, Judith. *Writing Local History.* Boise: Idaho State Historical Society, [publication pending].

A basic guide providing tips to people writing local history for publication.

Felt, Thomas E. *Researching, Writing, and Publishing Local History.* Nashville: AASLH, 1976.

The best book of its type, especially suitable to newcomers in researching, writing, and publishing.

Hale, Richard W., Jr. *Methods of Research for the Amateur Historian.* Technical Leaflet No. 21. Nashville: AASLH, 1969.

Basic tips on types of sources, where to find them, and how to organize notes. [Out of print.]

Kyvig, David E., and Myron A. Marty. *Nearby History: Exploring the Past Around You.* Nashville: AASLH, 1983.

A fine book on how to research local history and tie it in with national and international events. Discusses the use of published and unpublished records, artifacts, photographs, and oral history.

Reed, Mary E., and Carole Simon-Smolinski. *Researching Local History.* Boise: Idaho State Historical Society, 1985.

A basic guide for people just beginning historical research. Good analysis of resources available in all localities, from the common to the frequently overlooked.

Rikoon, J. Sanford. *Tradition Research as a Field for Community Studies.* Boise: Idaho State Historical Society, 1983.

A good basic guide detailing how a community's traditions can help in understanding community life. Sections on collecting and interpreting traditions.

Schlereth, Thomas J. *Artifacts and the American Past.* Nashville: AASLH, 1980.

Too often people researching local history rely only on written records. This book of essays explains how to utilize local architecture, the town's museum, photographs, and artifacts to interpret the past.

Weitzman, David. *Traces of the Past: A Field Guide to Industrial Archaeology.* New York: Charles Scribner's Sons, 1980. *Underfoot: An Everyday Guide to Exploring the American Past.* New York: Charles Scribner's Sons, 1976.

Perhaps more than any other author, Weitzman has produced in these two books works that can help make every person a historian. Excellent tips on how commonplace materials can be used to help interpret the past: tombstones, bridges, bottles, buildings, and many more. Highly recommended for teachers.

Exhibits

Baker, Charles L. *Planning Exhibits: From Concept to Opening.* Technical Leaflet No. 137. Nashville: AASLH, 1981.

Brief, basic information on planning and developing exhibits. [Out of print.]

Bowditch, George, and Holman J. Swinney. *Preparing Your Exhibits: Methods, Materials, and Bibliography.* Technical Leaflet No. 4. Nashville: AASLH, 1969. [Out of print.]

Neal, Arminta. *Exhibits for the Small Museum.* Nashville: AASLH, 1976. *Help for the Small Museum.* Nashville: AASLH, 1968.

The best books for those with little money who want to produce high-quality exhibits. Helpful information on design, labeling, lighting, and arrangement.

Family history

Helmhold, F. Wilbur. *Tracing Your Ancestry: A Step-by-Step Guide to Researching Your Family History.* Birmingham, Alabama: Oxmoor House, 1976.

Kotkin, Amy, et al. *Family Folklore: Interviewing Guide and Questionnaire.* Washington, D.C.: Smithsonian Institution, 1978.

A good guide for a new look at how to undertake a family history project.

Lichtman, Allan J. *Your Family History.* New York: Vintage Books, 1978.

Perhaps the best guide available for family historians. Chapters on oral history, written records, photographs, and methods of research. An excellent bibliography.

Shopes, Linda. *Using Oral History for a Family History Project.* Technical Leaflet No. 123. Nashville: AASLH, 1980.

[Out of print.]

Festivals

Reibel, Daniel. *Craft Festivals: A Planning Guide.* Technical Leaflet No. 117. Nashville: AASLH, 1979.

A good companion piece to the Wilson and Udall book cited below for those planning a crafts festival. [Out of print.]

Wilson, Joe, and Lee Udall. *Folk Festivals: A Handbook for Organization and Management.* Knoxville: University of Tennessee Press, 1982.

An excellent book which greatly details the amount of work and planning necessary to undertake a successful festival. Especially helpful sections on administration and publicity.

*Gathering and preserving: archives,
manuscripts, photographs, and oral history*

Baum, Willa K. *Oral History for the Local Historical Society.* Nashville: AASLH, 1971. *Transcribing and Editing Oral History.* Nashville: AASLH, 1977.

The best basic guides for those planning an oral history project. Cover such subjects as how to interview, ethics, equipment, preserving tapes, and transcription.

Conrad, James H. *Copying Historical Photographs: Equipment and Methods.* Technical Leaflet No. 139. Nashville: AASLH, 1981.

Tips on selecting a camera, making a copy stand, copying techniques, and storage. [Out of print.]

Davis, Cullom, Kathryn Back, and Kay MacLean. *Oral History: From Tape to Type.* Chicago: American Library Association, 1977.

Basic information on interviewing techniques, transcribing and research use.

Duckett, Kenneth W. *Modern Manuscripts: A Practical Manual for Their Management, Care, and Use.* Nashville: AASLH, 1975.

Discusses acquisition, conservation, and use of archival materials. A basic guide.

Ericson, Stacy. *A Field Guide for Oral History.* Boise: Idaho State Historical Society, 1981.

One of the best basic guides for those just beginning an oral history project. Includes sections on interviewing, funding, oral history in education, equipment, and so forth.

Ford, Karin E., and Beth Hilbert. *Local History in the Public Library: Starting and Building a Collection of Resources.* Boise: Idaho State Historical Society, 1985.

A basic guide for groups wanting to organize a local history research collection.

Thompson, Enid T. *Local History Collections: A Manual for Librarians.* Nashville: AASLH, 1978.

Probably the most basic book to assist with the preservation of local history research materials.

Weinstein, Robert A., and Larry Booth. *Collection, Use, and Care of Historical Photographs.* Nashville: AASLH, 1977.

The most comprehensive book on collecting, preserving, and storing historical photographs.

Historic preservation; architectural survey projects

Attebery, Jennifer Eastman. *Documenting Historic Buildings.* Boise: Idaho State Historical Society, 1985.

A basic guide to researching, photographing, and recording historic buildings. Especially useful to people planning historic-site survey projects.

Blumenson, John J-G. *Identifying American Architecture: A Pictorial Guide to Styles and Terms, 1600-1945.* Revised edition. Nashville: AASLH, 1982.

More than 200 photographs help users identify basic American architectural styles. A useful guide for those undertaking site survey projects.

Historic preservation brochures. The following can be obtained at no cost from the Department of the Interior, National Park Service, Washington, D.C. 20240, or from your State Historic Preservation Office:

The National Register of Historic Places

The Secretary of the Interior's Standards for Rehabilitation

Tax Incentives for Rehabilitating Historic Buildings

Munsell, Kenneth, ed. *Historic Preservation Resourcebook for Small Communities.* Ellensburg, Washington: Small Towns Institute, 1983.

A general guidebook to historic preservation efforts in small towns throughout the United States. Numerous articles and case studies on promotion, signage, historic building tours, tourism, and financing. [Available from Small Towns Institute, Box 517, Ellensburg, Washington 98926.]

Swanson, Ann. *A Role for the Private Citizen in Historic Preservation.* Boise: Idaho State Historical Society, 1985.

A basic guide to grass-roots involvement in historic preservation.

Watts, Donald W. *Using Main Street: Historic Preservation in Your Downtown.* Boise: Idaho State Historical Society, 1985.

A basic guide for groups interested in downtown revitalization.

Ziegler, Arthur P., and Walter C. Kidney. *Historic Preservation in Small Towns.* Nashville: AASLH, 1980.

A practical sourcebook to help people in small towns preserve community buildings. Helpful case studies and a good bibliography.

Museums and historical societies

Creigh, Dorothy Weyer. *A Primer for Local Historical Societies.* Nashville: AASLH, 1976.

Along with the Silvestro book mentioned below, this is the basic guide for those wishing to organize a local historical society. Tips on pre-organization planning, financing, volunteers, and so forth. Good grass-roots approach.

Guthe, Carl E. *The Management of Small History Museums.* Nashville: AASLH, 1977.

Although the first edition is nearly thirty years old, this is still an indispensable handbook for those thinking of organizing a museum.

Harrison, Raymond O. *The Technical Requirements of Small Museums.* Technical Paper No. 1. Ottawa: Canadian Museums Association, 1966. This short book (27 pages) is the best yet published for outlining the space requirements necessary for a successful museum. It is highly recommended for any group that is thinking of building a new building or remodeling an old one as a community museum. [Out of print.]

Lord, Barry, and Gail Dexter Lord, eds. *Planning Our Museums.* Ottawa: National Museums of Canada, 1983. A good companion piece to the Harrison booklet cited above. One of the few guides to architectural considerations for those planning a museum — whether in a new building or in a renovated old one.

Silvestro, Clement M. *Organizing a Local Historical Society.* Nashville: AASLH, 1975. A helpful guide for communities hoping to establish a historical society.

Publishing

Felt, Thomas E. *Researching, Writing, and Publishing Local History.* Nashville: AASLH, 1976.

Purcell, L. Edward. *Writing Printing Specifications: A Systematic Approach to Publications Management.* Technical Leaflet No. 142. Nashville: AASLH, 1981. Helpful information on how to write bid specifications for printers. [Out of print.]

School and youth projects

Bancroft, Barbara, comp. *Teaching Idaho History with Folk Arts: A Compilation of Teachers' Ideas.* Boise: Idaho State Department of Education, 1979. A helpful booklet describing what folk arts are, how folk artists can be located even in small communities, and how these people can help students learn and appreciate history.

Hoopes, James. *Oral History: An Introduction for Students.* Chapel Hill: University of North Carolina Press, 1979. A comprehensive guide with an excellent bibliography.

Metcalf, Fay D., and Matthew T. Downey. *Using Local History in the Classroom.* Nashville: AASLH, 1982.

Probably the first book of its type, this is recommended for grade 7 and above. Details how to find local historical resources in the community; use local history in the study of family, economic, social, or political history; and develop projects.

Sitton, Thad, George L. Mehaffy, and O. L. Davis, Jr. *Oral History: Projects for Teachers (and Others)*. Austin: University of Texas Press, 1983.

This manual is primarily for public school teachers but is also suitable for college-level instruction.

Your Classroom and the Bicentennial. Helena: Montana Bicentennial Administration, [1975?].

An excellent handbook for teachers, with hundreds of school project ideas — not only for history classes but also for art, science, vocational, music, foreign language, and other students. Perhaps the best "idea" book for school projects. [Out of print.]

Slide-tape and videotape programs

Jolly, Brad. *Videotaping Local History*. Nashville: AASLH, 1982.

A concise work which makes an argument that videotaping is very affordable. Written for those with no previous experience, the book's primary strength is its detailed examination of video equipment.

Smith, Arthur L. *Producing the Slide Show for Your Historical Society*. Technical Leaflet No. 42. Nashville: AASLH, 1967.

[Out of print.]

PUBLICITY AND PUBLIC RELATIONS

Adams, G. Donald. *Working Effectively with the Press: A Guide for Historical Societies*. Technical Leaflet No. 142. Nashville: AASLH, 1980.

Excellent practical advice on writing news releases and garnering other types of publicity. [Out of print.]

Brigham, Nancy. *How to do Leaflets, Newsletters and Newspapers*. Sommerville, Massachusetts: New England Free Press, 1976.

[Available from New England Free Press, 60 Union Square, Sommerville, Massachusetts 02143.]

Derby, Charlotte S. *Reaching Your Public: The Historical Society Newsletter*. Technical Leaflet No. 39. Nashville: AASLH, 1967.

Good pointers on the types of information to include in a newsletter and how to make one look attractive. [Out of print.]

Gignilliat, Marguerite. *Reaching Your Public Through the Newspaper.* Technical Leaflet No. 45. Nashville: AASLH, 1968. [Out of print.]

Hansen, Phoebe J. *Publicity: A Guide for Public Humanities Projects.* Minneapolis: Federation of Public Programs in the Humanities, n.d..

A short but very helpful guide. Details planning, knowing your audience, and preparing a publicity schedule. Also includes sample news releases and public service announcements. [Available from National Federation of State Humanities Councils, 12 S. 6th St., Suite 527, Minneapolis, Minnesota 55402.]

If You Want Air Time. Washington, D.C.: National Association of Broadcasters, 1974.

[Available from National Association of Broadcasters, 1771 N St., N.W., Washington, D.C. 20036.]

Pattison, Polly, and Mark Beach. *60 Ways to Save Money on Newsletters.* Portland, Oregon: Coast-to-Coast Books, 1983.

This short brochure is useful to any group thinking of printing newsletters, posters, catalogs, brochures, or practically anything else. [Available from Coast-to-Coast Books, 2934 N.E. 16th Ave., Portland, Oregon 97212.]

Publicity Handbook: A Guide for Publicity Chairmen. Fort Worth, Texas: Sperry & Hutchinson Co., 1972.

[Available from Consumer Services, Sperry & Hutchinson Co., 2900 West Seminary Dr., Fort Worth, Texas 76133.]

Successful Public Relations Techniques. San Francisco: Public Management Institute, n.d.

Includes information on creating newsworthy events, getting key people to support your work, dealing effectively with the media, and using public relations to expand your funding base. Expensive. [Available from Public Management Institute, 333 Hayes St., San Francisco, California 94102.]

Wheeler, Robert. *Effective Public Relations: Communicating Your Image.* Technical Leaflet No. 3. Nashville: AASLH, 1973.

Tips on timing, selecting a public relations officer, promoting your organization. [Out of print.]